I0425745

Little John' s Writing

Preface

Little John is an oversea Chinese. He was born close to the end of the Sino-Japanese war (1944). About 3 years old, he went to Taiwan with his parents, he grew up there and received education up to college. In 1967, he arrived in USA to pursuit graduate study. Then, he found a job, became a citizen of USA, have family, and retired (2011).

Little John received education in Taiwan, which teaches traditional Chinese Confucianism, learned Chinese history, Dr. Sun Yatsen's political doctrine – The three principles for the people. At high school, little John believed Jesus, but his understanding of Jesus is much later, in 1989. Chinese history of 19-20 century told every Chinese, China was humiliated and bullied, Chinese were killed, by the strong foreign countries; Chinese people killed each other; but China gradually stood up from poverty and behind. To little John's amazement, after the Reform and Opening in 1978, after 40 years, China not only stands up, it becomes a strong nation in the world, can not be ignored. Little John is touched by this fact and starts to study the world history. This book is the result of his study, his understanding and questions of our world (mainly China and USA).

Little John is a Christian. This book analyzes our world from a Christian's point of view. Little John believes God created the universe and everything in it. The fate of every race, nation, and person are in God's hand, no matter you know God or not. God already told us the ending of our world. He also told us how to live. But most people do not put God's advice in their mind, they do what they want to do. God let people have freedom to choose his/her way of living, but God also told us He will judge us by what we did.

Notes:
1. This book's ISBN numbers are ISBN-13: 9781086158342.
2. This book has copyright protection.
3. This book is owned and published by Ten Books, Inc.
4. Please forward any comment to this e-mail address: feiyugospel44@gmail.com.

Acknowledgement Author thanks God to let this book be written.
Frank Yu, Editor, Ten Books, Inc.   August 30, 2019

He also wants to dedicate this book to his wife, Sophia Kay-Shan, his family: Joseph and Mary, Miles and Dylan; James and Rachel, Ava and Emma.

Author Frank Yu was born in China, grew up in Taiwan, China. His specialty is process design. After he retired in Jan. 2011, he spent more time in teaching ESL, translation, and writing.

Table of Content

Chapter 1 2018 Election of Local ROC Public Officials

2018 left; 2019 arrives. To the people grew up in Taiwan, there was a big event happened in 2018 in Taiwan. It will affect Taiwam's future. The event is the ROC (Republic of China) local election of its public officials on November 24, 2018. It is a big election in Taiwan for 6 municipality mayors, 3 city mayors, and 13 county heads; total 22 positions.

I. Background

The three major political powers in Taiwan are: Kuomintang (KMT), Democratic Progressive Party (DPP), and non-partisans. In 2014's local public official election, DPP had a big win, won 13 positions, whereas KMT won 6 positions. In 2016 presidential election, DPP's Tsai Ing-wen was elected. DPP advocates independence of Taiwan and is hostile to China. KMT advocates peaceful unification of Taiwan with China, same as China and most oversea Chinese. Unification of Taiwan and China is a major task and historical responsibility of China. There is no other choice. If necessary, China will use force to accomplish this task. Therefore, if DDP is in control, there is possibility of war between the two sides, but if KMT is in control, peaceful unification is possible. [1]

In 2016, after DPP took over of the government, it is hostile to China, attacks KMT, and practises its policies to remove the influence of China (such as removing the statues of President Chiang, revising textbook to minimize teach anything about China, etc.). China also starts not to buy goods from Taiwan, not to travel in Taiwan, but welcomes local native to work in China. After 2 years, the economy of Taiwan has problems, especially for tourist business and fruit producers; but many natives go to work in China.

II. The result of 2018 local public official election

The result of 2018 local public official election was KMT had a big win ; they won 15 positions, whereas DPP won 6 positions. This election shows people don't like DPP. We also see the courage of KMT candidates, willing to stand up and challenge DPP, struggle to fight for the peace of Taiwan. [R1]

The result of mayor election in Kaohsiung is a surprise to everyone. In tradition (during the past 20 years), Koahsiung located at southern Taiwan is DPP's turf for the local natives. During this election, KMT's candidate is Han Kuo-yu, a second generation from China. Mr. Han didn't have lots money for his election. It seems impossible for him to be elected, but Mr. Han decided to participate in this election and his election slogan is to respect the 1992 consensus reached for the both sides of China [2], which means peaceful unification of Taiwan and China, and to develop business between two sides of China. For the 2018 election, Mr. Han is the only candidate using 1992 consensus as election slogan. Per public poll of April 2018, Mr. Han's support lacking DPP candidate about 10-20%；in September, the poll showed Mr. Han's support is 32%, DPP candidate's support is 34%；in October/November, the poll showed Mr. Han's support is 10% more than his DPP opponent (48% vs 38%). The result of this election was: 892,525 votes (53.9%) for Mr. Han；his DPP opponent had 742,239 votes (44.8%). Han Kuo-yu was elected as mayor of Kaohsiung.

III. The meaning of 2018 local public official election

This election shows people in Taiwan are not interested in independence, fighting with mainland China, not agree with the policy of DPP, but more concern about the economy in Taiwan and the future peace in Taiwan. Their hope just like anyone in this world – have enough food for the family and have a peaceful life.

The 2018 local public official election is a turning point for the political struggle in Taiwan, but DPP will not give up, it will use various means hoping to continue its power and influence. The next important election in Taiwan is the 2020 presidential election. From now on to this election, we will see many political activities. What we see are: DPP's continuation in power will cause further economy downturn in Taiwan, may lead to war with mainland China; only DPP will gain (power/wealth), while people suffer. What Taiwan needs are: more economic development/prosperity and peace. The choice is not to let DPP continue in power. We don't need another war between China and Taiwan. We need peace and good life.

IV. God's word

God told us there is struggle of justice and evil. People has his/her freedom to choose his/her way of living, but God will judge us based on our behavior – by reward or punishment. No one will escape God's judgement. God also told us, one day this world will be perished, a new world will come, there will be no war, everyone will respect God, obey God's command and live a happy peaceful life with God. God! Hope your kingdom will come soon.

Notes:
1. The official name of the government in Taiwan is 'Republic of China'. It has 23.57 million people. Its presidents are: Chiang Kai-shek(蔣中正) (1948-1974), Yen Chia-kan(严家淦) (1975-1978)，Chiang Ching-kuo(蔣经国) (1978-1988), Lee Teng-hui(李登辉) (1989-2000), Chen Shui-bian(

陈水扁) (2000-2008)，Ma Ying-jeou(马英九) (2008-2016)，蔡英文
(Tsai Ing-wen) (2016-现在)。(See website: https://zh.wikipedia.org/wiki/
中華民國總統) Per Chinese custom, a person's name started with its
surname and followed by its regular name. There is no middle name.
2. 1992 consensus: It is referred to the meeting in November, 1992,
between Association for Relations Across the Taiwan Straits (from
mainland China) and Straits Exchange Foundation (from Taiwan) reached
a common ground of one China among Taiwan and mainland China, for
the purpose to resolve issues among these two organizations. (See website:
https://zh.wikipedia.org/wiki/九二共識)

Reference:
1. See website: https://zh.wikipedia.org/wiki/2018 年中華民國直轄市長
及縣市長選舉

Chapter 2 Style of Government

When we examine the style of government of a nation, we find there are many different ones. Basically, there is no nation is pure socialism or capitalism; most of them are mainly capitalism with socialism or mainly socialism with capitalism. Besides these, there are few nations still have king ruling over the people; but now most kings are only symbolic, without political power. Based on the power of making law, most nations are either using democratic congress or relied on dictatorship; country's head is president, prime minister, or chairman, by election or appointment. In this chapter, different government styles in history and now are presented.

I. Three ancient government styles

In ancient, many tribes had a leader to rule over them, just like a king. In history, we find three unusual ruling styles: The first one happened in Israel. God was the ruler. The second one happened in China. A capable person ruled over people. The third one happened in Greece, a democratic government based on people was in power.

I.1 God ruled over people

In history, people were once ruled by God.

I.1.1 God selected Israelites

According to the Old Testament, around 2100 BC, God chose Abraham, a righteous person in God's view. God made a covenant with Abraham: If Abraham's offspring obey God's command, God will give them the land at Canaan and they will be God's people and receive God's blessings, but if they disobey God's command, they will be punished by God.

In 1876 BC, God used Joseph, an offspring of Abraham and Egypt's prime minister, brought his family of 70 people to Egypt to escape famine. [1] After 400 years, they multiplied and became a race – Israelites. Egyptians treated Israelites as slaves. Israelites prayed to God for help. God selected Moses to lead Israelites out of Egypt. When Moses made a request to Pharaoh to let Israelites to leave Egypt, Pharaoh refused. God punished Egypt using 10 plagues. Finally, in 1446 BC, Pharaoh agreed to let Israelites to leave Egypt. At this time, Israelites had 600 thousand male soldiers above 20 years old. After Israelites left, Pharaoh regretted and sent all his troops to bring Israelites back, but God protected Israelites. God parted the water at the Red Sea to let Israelites across the sea, but after the Israelites across the sea, God let the water merged and killed the Egyptian soldiers. [2]

After Israelites left Egypt, God gave manna and quails to Israelites as food. Three months later, they arrived Mount Sinai. God appeared to Israelites at Mount Sinai; there were thunders, lightings, dark clouds, sound of horns at the mountain. [3] God gave Moses Ten Commandments and laws, to be given to Israelites. God also told Moses how to make Tabernacle to worship God. On January 1, the 2nd year Israelites left Egypt, God's Tabernacle was set up. The cloud and God's glory filled the Tabernacle. From this day on, when the cloud lifted above the Tabernacle, Israelites would set out; otherwise they would stay. During the day, God's cloud would stay at the Tabernacle; at evening, there were fire from the cloud to light up the sky. [4]

I.1.2 The failure and punishment of Israelites

On February 20, the 2nd year after the Israelites left Egypt, God led Israelites left Mount Sinai to Canaan. On the way, Israelites complained the hardship of their life and made God angry at them. When they arrived at the border of Canaan, God told Moses to send 12 spies, one from each Israelite's tribe, to Canaan to check the local conditions. After 40 days, the spies came back. They all agreed that Canaan is a good place full of honey and milk, but 10 of the spies didn't agree they should go to occupy Canaan, because they thought the people lived there were stronger than they and their city was protected by strong walls; only 2 spies (Joshua and Caleb) suggested to occupy Canaan, because God would help them. Israelites agreed with the 10 spies, not willing to occupy Canaan. This made God very angry. God punished Israelites would wander in the desert for 40 years; anyone was above 20 years old and disagreed to occupy Canaan would die in the desert, not able to enter Canaan. [5] Israelites' fate was carried out as what God said.

I.1.3 Israelites occupied Canaan

40 years later, God told Moses to lead Israelites into Canaan. Moses led Israelites occupied the land at east of the Jordan River and died at Mount Nebo, east of the Jordan River. Before Moses' death, he arranged Joshua to be Israelites' leader per God's command. [6] After Moses' death (in 1406 BC), Joshua led Israelites occupied Canaan, west of the Jordan River. [7] After the death of Joshua in 1380 BC, Israelites continued to occupy more land in Canaan; but because they didn't eliminate all the native tribes and their idols, God didn't help them to eliminate all the native tribes. Israelites started a period of Judges (1380-1050 BC). When Israelites were away from God, God put Israelites in the hand of some native tribe. When Israelites prayed to God for help, God raised a judge to help Israelites. The last Judge of Israelites was Samuel. When Samuel was old, Israelites asked him to set up a king for them, as their surrounding countries. Samuel asked God. God accepted the Israelites' request. This ended God's direct ruling over Israelites.

I.2 Abdication in China

In ancient China, there were two leaders, similar to king. They didn't pass their position to their son, but to a more capable person. This is abdication. They were Yao and Shun.

About 3000 BC, there were some tribes lived at the middle and downstream area of Yellow River. The first recorded leader was Huang Di (Di means emperor in Chinese). His ruling was from 2690 to 2590 BC. After Huang Di (黄帝), Yao (尧) became the tribe leader, after his father Diku (帝喾). Yao lived a simple life. He lived in a simple cottage, ate simple food, and wore linen clothes. Yao was good at handling issues and was not afraid to suffer together with his people. He ruled about 100 years (2333-2234 BC). When he was old, he recognized that his son was not suitable to be a leader; so he started to look for someone to take over his position. He found Shun (舜), a person with good moral and ability. After a period of observation, he decided to abdicate his position to Shun. Shun ruled about 50 years (2233-2184 BC). During the time of Yao and Shun, there was flooding problem from the Yellow River. Yao asked Gun to tame the flooding. Gun used the method of blockage but failed after tried for 9 years. Shun asked Gun's son, Yu (禹), to tame the flooding. Yu used the method of unblocking. After 13 years of trying, Yu solved the flooding problem. Yu worked very hard in taming the flooding. Three times, he passed his home, but he didn't go home. Yu's work of taming the flooding was greatly appreciated and Shun decided to abdicate his leadership to Yu. These were the two abdication in Chinese history. [8, 9]

I.3 Democrate government in ancient Greece [10, 11]

In 507 BC, Greece Athens leader Cleisthenes developed a democratic government to serve people. He set up three departments to manage Greece's affairs: 1) Citizens Assembly (The Ekklesia): to decide internal affairs, diplomatic issues, appoint/remove officials, etc.; met once every 10 days; meeting result was decided by voting; it is equivalent to a congress. Any male citizen 18 years old were eligible to participate this meeting. 2) Council (The Boule): to handle daily Greece internal and external affairs; to decide the meeting agenda of Citizens Assembly; it was an executive department, met daily. It was made by 500 people, selected from Athens' 10 tribes, with one-year term; it was divided into 10 groups, taking turns to handle business. 3) Jury Court: Athens had 10 courts to handle litigation cases; it was a judiciary department. There were 6000 jurors. Each court had 500 jurors, with the remaining 1000 jurors as spares. Juror was selected by casting lots, with one-year term, not allowed to be reselected. Any male citizen over 30 years old were eligible to be a juror.

This old democratic government system was practiced in Greece for two centuries. It ended when Alexander the Great took the power. It inspired the current democratic governing system.

II. Other government styles in history

Most ancient government styles are dictator ruling by a king or tribe chief; it is a feudal society. For a long time (5-18 century), Europe was ruled by kings and religious leaders, political and religious powers were combined to rule a nation. [12] In 1792, a democratic revolution happened in France. In January 1793, French king, Louis XVI, was killed at guillotine and France became a democratic republic. [13] From this time on, more countries become democratic republic and monarchy was going downhill. [14]

In 1764, Watt in England improved and invented steam engine. People started to use machine instead of human to make products. It started an industrial revolution and created capitalists and labors. The contradict interests of the capitalist and labor generate capitalism, imperialism, socialism, and communism. As regard to government style, there are democratic congress, constitutional monarchy, dictatorship, and monarchy.

II.1 Capitalism

Capitalism is a doctrine about a nation's economic system and mode of production. It has following features: [15]

1. Capital: Use capital to make products or service. The purpose is to make profit.
2. Personal property: People are allowed to own property; including factory to make products or company to provide service.
3. Price: Price of a product or service is depended on the supply and demand of the market.

The advantages of capitalism are: 1. In order to make profit, businessmen will try to improve their products, created new product or service. These help improvement in a society. 2. Competition among businessmen will help reduce product's price and benefit the consumers. 3. It provides jobs in a society.

The disadvantages of capitalism are: 1. Some businessman may control the market to make others hard to compete with him/her. 2. In order to make profit, business will reduce labor's salary, creating hardship for the labors; or cut corners to reduce the price of a product, or making fake product, causing problems to consumers. 3. Rich become richer and poor become poorer. 4. The poor business management will cause loss or bankrupcy of a company. In more serious cases, it will cause economic panic and unemployment in a society, such as the big depression of USA in 1929-1939.

A capitalism country without control, sometimes, will have problems. Therefore, in many capitalism countries, government will oversee its business activities; such as not to allow monopoly to happen in a business, government will help the poors, oversee the stock market activities, etc. These actions are provided to prevent problems in economy. The difference is different country has their own way to handle the issues.

II.2 Imperialism

Imperialism exists since ancient times. It was there for a nation to expand territory or resolve issues. Any nation who was defeated, its people would be killed or became slaves. In ancient China, from Han Dynasty (206 BC), China treated some neighbor countries as subordinates at 4 different levels. For the closest subordinate country, China would ordain its king, provide protection, received gifts to the emperor, but it would manage its own affairs inside its kingdom. During Qing dynasty, Korea, Okinawa, Vietnam (including Laos and Cambodia), were China's closest subordinate countries. This policy of China was to have peaceful relationship with its neighboring countries. It also served for its own protection. In Chapter 3, more Chinese history is presented. Mencius

In 18th century, industrial revolution happened in Europe. In 19th century, many European countries, such as British, French, Germany, Netherlands, Spain, Portugal, Italy, etc., became fully developed industrial nations. They used machine in production. Their weapon was not sword, but gun. They had ships and trains. Their military was very strong. In Africa, Asia, and America, they found people could be their slaves [17]; some places having resources they could use; some places they could sell their products. Therefore, they used their strong military force to help them sell slaves, set up colonies, sell their products, sign treaties in their favor to make money. They became imperialism. Besides these European countries, Japan in Asia and USA in America also became imperialism. Japan went to the extreme. It not only invaded China, but it hoped to rule the whole Asia. In Chapter 4 and 5, more history of USA and Japan are presented.

The imperialism of 19th and 20th century was the dark record in human history, nothing good about it. It showed sin of human, violated the God's teaching about justice and loving people.

World War II (WWII) was a war between justice and evil. At end of this war, Axis countries were defeat and Allies won. [18] Japan lost its dream to rule the whole Asia and control of many nations. After the war, colonies of British and other European countries were independent. British no longer can claim the sun never set in its territory.

After WW II, the situation of the world was changed. The world was divided to two camps: free and democratic countries and communism countries. This was the period of cold war, from 1947 to 1991 AD. [19] the head of the free democratic countries was USA. After WWII, the prestige of USA in the world reached its peak. It became the strongest country in the world, but unfortunately, it wanted to be the hegemon of the world, behaved like an imperialism, lacking the justice of God's teaching. The leader of the communism countries is Soviet Union. These two groups of countries fought each other, on the table or under the table. After the disintegration of the Soviet Union in 1991, the fighting continues.

II.3 Socialism

Socialism is a concept for an ideal society in our world. This concept happened in ancient times. In 380 BC, Plato wrote a book, "Republic", discussed the ideal society. [20] In China, Confucius (孔子;551-479 BC) mentioned an ideal world in his writing. In his ideal world, people elect wise and capable people to manage affairs in a nation; people treated each other with peace, love, and trust; everyone (man, woman, old, young, widow, widower, and handicapped) will be taken care of. Therefore, there is no evil plots and theft, people are safe, even his/her door can be left open at night. [21]

The socialism of 19th century claimed: 1) There is no class difference among people. 2) There is no rich or poor difference among people. 3) Production tools are owned and used by the public. 4) Everyone makes his/her contribution and takes what he/she needs; serve each other as a happy community. [22; page 32]

As regard to the means of carryout socialism, there are many ways, range from the mild one without violence to the communism using violence.

II.4 Communism [22]

Communism is one type of socialism. It advocates using force/violence to overthrow the capitalists and gain the political power. Its founder is Karl Max, a German philosopher. In 19th century, science helped people have many new discoveries. People understood the universe better. New discoveries helped people improve their life. Max thought he had a scientific explanation of human society. He claimed economy of a society determines everything in a society. Therefore, to change a society, we should start with its economic structure. This is materialism. Marx also thought he discovered a law for the human history. He claimed that human history is a history of struggle among the classes. This is dialectics. Marx used his theory to forecast the changes of future society as follows: Due to the exploitation of the capitalists to the labors, the society will have the rich people and the poor people. Eventually, the society will collapse. Proletariat will rise to defeat the capitalists to set up a socialism country. At this time, the capitalists may want to restore their control. Therefore, it is important to teach people to practice proletariat dictatorship; to eliminate the classes in the society and form a society of communism. The special traits of a communism country are dictatorship, one-party dictatorship, enterprises owned by states, control people's freedom of speech, atheism.

In November 1917, the Communism Party in Russia overthrew the Czar (the Russian Empire) and founded the first country of communism, the Soviet Union. In Soviet Union, enterprises were owned by government, people were lack of motivation to work. The society was poor, not prosper. People didn't have enough daily necessities. After 1960/1970, the life of ruling class in Soviet Union was corrupted and caused discontents among people. In 1980's, USA lowered the price of oil and caused economic loss for Soviet Union. In 1985, Gobachev became the leader in Soviet Union. He carried out two policies. One was to let market to decide what to produce and develop, and the other was to let people have more freedom of speech. His new policies speeded up the disintegration of Soviet Union. In 1991, people using the new power to end the ruling of Soviet Union. Soviet Union was disintegrated into 15 countries. [23]

China is another communism country. In 1949, Chinese Communism Party seized power in China. It practiced communism in China, but just like Soviet Union, its economy and people's living standard didn't improve. In 1978, Deng Xiaoping implemented "reform and opening up" policy in China. Basically, it allows individual to do business, while the government is handling other business. [24] This reform is very successful. After 40 years, China not only becomes rich and strong, it becomes a world power, can not be ignored.

History already showed the defects and mistakes of communism. Communism predicts capitalism will be broken one day, but history tells us

capitalism after some revision, still exists. For this reason, the violence used by communism and proletariat dictatorship may not be necessary. It is very interesting to observe that during proletariat dictatorship, the people used to own property become proletariat and people used to be proletariat start to own property. Communism ignored the sinful nature and selfish of human, which cause depression of their economy and lacking daily necessities. Besides these, the Evolution Theory and the Athesim promoted by Communism are basically wrong.

Most people lived in a poor area will support Communism, because Communism advocate to reverse the wealth distribution and everyone has food to eat. They overlook the fact that under communism's ruling, everyone will live a poor life and without freedom.

II.5 Democracy and dictatorship
There are basically two government styles: democratic congress system and dictatorship system. In democratic congress system, people elect president and congressman/congresswoman to rule the country. People use

election to prove or disapprove policy of a country. Most capitalism countries adopt democratic congress system for their country. In dictatorship system, a dictator or a group of dictators rules the country, decides the country's policy; people's duty is to obey. In fact, in today's dictatorship country, people will have meetings to discuss issues of the country, but the final decision is in the hand of the dictator. Most communism countries are under dictatorship system.

The advantages of democratic congress system are: 1) The minority obeys the majority. It is a reasonably solution. 2) During election, especially when there is some big issue, after some debates, people are able to understand how to make his/her vote. 3) This process can be repeated forever. Its disadvantages are: 1) Some elected officials are serving for themselves or some special interest group. It is not fair. It is a corruption. 2) When there is no big issue in election, it is hard for people to understand which candidate is good or bad. Many people will choose not to vote. Some may make mistakes to vote the wrong person. 3) To change an issue or to remove an official from office, people must wait for the next election, which usually is 2 to 4 years later.

The advantage of dictatorship system is very efficient, but its disadvantages are: 1) If the dictator is incompetent or corrupt, it will damage the nation. 2) It is not easy to change a dictator. 3) A dictator has limited life span.

Democratic congress system and dictatorship system are created by human to rule a country. They like other human invention, have advantages and disadvantages, but not perfect. As long as human's sinful nature exists, neither democracy nor dictatorship is a perfect government system, because either system will cause problem.

III. People and nation

The hope of most people is to be able to live a peaceful life: have a job to support family, have enough food to eat, have clothes to keep warm, have a place to live, have vehicle to travel from one place to another, children have opportunity to be educated, elders have someone to take care of; there is justice in a society. As regards to which government system to be used perhaps is a secondary consideration, not very important. Many times, in fact, people have no choice of which system to be used in his/her country.

When we look the history, we find that the reason that people riseup to overthrow a government is due to not able to live (no food to eat) or/and to be treated unreasonably. History teaches us that people's patience has its limit. Over this limit, people will riseup to fight against the government.

It is a government's job to serve its people. It is also a government's job to manage (control) its people. Therefore, a government and its people sometimes are at opposite positions. The ideal situation is people are willing to accept government's control. To reach this situation, a government should pay attention to whether its control of people is fair, acceptable to people or not. In China, there was a story of Zhuge Liang: he arrested Meng Huo seven times to make Meng Huo obeyed him willingly. [25] This story told us that it is important that government's control to its people is fair, so that people are willing to accept its control. Otherwise, problems will happen.

The standard to judge a government should be based on it is really serving its people or not, its people are willing to accept its control or not; not based on what system it is used. The concept that people are more important than a nation or monarh was mentioned about in 4th century BC in China by Mencius (孟子), a master of Confucianism after Confucius. [26]

IV. Relationship between nations

A government besides managing internal affairs, it also makes contacts with other nations, because it is impossible for a nation to be self sufficient, it needs to trade and communicate with other nations. The relationship between nations should be equal, mutually beneficial, respect each other, not to interfere other nation's internal affairs, justice and reasonable. Otherwise, there will be problems.

Colonialism and imperialism are policies to invade and sieze resources of other nations. The victims will not accept the mistreatment, resistance can not be avoided. History already proves the mistakes of colonialism and imperialism. After WWII, colonialism disappeared, but imperialism still exists. Forcing others to obey with military force will make people angry and will not be accepted. An unjustice and unreasonable diplomacy will not be accepted by anyone.

V. God's word

Bible is God's word for us. Bible tells us human are sinful, easy to commit sin, making mistakes. Our experience tells us that our ability and wisdom are limited. From Bible, we see the mighty power of God, His justice and love for human.

There is no god in this world claims that it created the universe, but the God in the Bible did. God created our ancestors. He is our ancestors' parents. He is also our parents. The relationship between us and God are very close, not far away. The mighty God told us He wants to be our friend. No matter you know Him or not, we are under His authority, and our future is in His hand.

Now, people rule over the world, but Bible tells us, one day God will rule over the world. God will give everyone a new heart and let everyone know Him. God! Hope your kingdom will come soon.

God's word: [Bible verses from Old Testament (ERV, Standard version)]

Isaiah 45:22 So all you people in faraway places, turn to me and be saved for I am God, and there is no other.
Ezekiel 38:23 Then I will show how great I am. I will prove that I am holy. Many nations will see me do these things, and they will learn who I am. Then they will know that I am the LORD.
Malachi 1:11 For from the rising of the sun to its setting, my name will be great among the nations; in every place, incense and pure offering will be offered to my name. For my name will be great among the nations, says the Lord of hosts.

Notes:
1. See Old Testament, the Book of Genesis, Chapter 12-50.
2. See Old Testament, the Book of Exodus, Chapter 1-14.
3. See Old Testament, the Book of Exodus, Chapter 15-19. In Ch. 19, Bible described in detail about God came down at Mount Sinai. It is a rare event happened in this world.
4. See Old Testament, the Book of Ecodus, Chapter 20-40. God's cloud and fire column are rare scenes in this world.
5. See Old Testament, the Book of Numbers, Chapter 10-14.
6. See Old Testament, the Book of Numbers, Chapter 33; Deuteronomy Chapter 2-3, 31, 34.
7. See Old Testament, the Book of Joshua, Chapter 1-13.
8. Mandarin Daily News Dictionary (国语日报辞典); 1st publication in Dec. 1974; by Mandarin Daily News Publication; Taiwan, China.
9. Story of Yao, Shun, and Yu, see website:
https://wenku.baidu.com/view/1e37d41f2279168888486d7f0.html?sxts=1552601172741
10. Ancient Greek Democracy (古希腊的民主), see website:
https://www.history.com/topics/ancient-greece/ancient-greece-democracy
11. Democrate system of ancient Greece (古代希腊民主制度), see website:
https://wenku.baidu.com/view/8a7a442e2f3f5727a5e9856a561252d380eb20ff.html?rec_flag=default&sxts=1553035410350
12. History of Europe (欧洲的历史), see website:
https://en.wikipedia.org/wiki/History_of_Europe
13. French Revoluntionary Wars (法国革命战争), see website:
https://en.wikipedia.org/wiki/French_Revolutionary_Wars
14. History of democracy (民主的历史), see website:

https://en.wikipedia.org/wiki/History_of_democracy

15. Capitalism (资本主义), see website: https://en.wikipedia.org/wiki/Capitalism
A joke of capitalism: One day, a news reporter asked the America oil tycoon, John Rockfeller, "How much more money you have will satisfy you?" John thought about the question. Finally, he said, "Just a little bit more."

16. A study of ancient China's subordinate system for foreign country (古代中国藩属体制的探索), see website:
https://wenku.baidu.com/view/d49dda8a90c69ec3d5bb75aa.html?from=search
https://wenku.baidu.com/view/75756b2da5e9856a56126051.html?from=search

17. In 18th and 19th century, European captured black people in west Africa and sold them as slaves. In 19th century, they decided abolishing this practice. In order to solve the problem of labor, they hired or tricked many Chinese to Europe and north/south America to be coolies.

18. During WWII, the Axis countries are: Germany, Italy, and Japan; Allies are: China, USA, United Kingdom, Frence, Netherlands, Belgium, Denmark, Greece, Poland, Norway, Yogoslavia, South Africa, New Zeland, Australia, Brizil, and Canada.

19. After WWII, the world was divided to two camps, as follows:
Free democratic countries: USA, United Kingdom, Frence, West Germany, Netherlands, Belgium, Denmark, Greece, Norway, South Africa, New Zeland, Australia, South Korea, Brizil, and Canada.
Communism countries: Soviet Union, China, Poland, East Germany, Czech Republic, Hungary, Romania, Bulgaria, Albania, North Korea, North Vietnam, Afghan, Mongolia, Cuba, Nigaragua, Yemen, Angola, and Ethiopia.

20. Republic, author: Plato, a Greece philosopher. It was written in 380 BC. He used the dialogue of Socrates, his teacher, to describe the utopia vision of an ideal society. He mentioned there are three types of people in an ideal society: ruler, specialized in management; warrior, specialized in protection; and people, specialized in production. See website:
https://en.wikipedia.org/wiki/Republic_(Plato)

21. Confucius in his writing "The great unity when everyone practices courtesy" (礼运大同篇) described his utopia vision of an ideal society, as follows: When the big way (of living) opens up, the world belongs to all the people (no fighting, greedy, and selfish), people elect wise and capable people to manage affairs in the nation; people treated each other with peace, love, and trust; everyone (man, woman, old, young, widow, widower, and handicapped) will be taken care of; every men has his duty and every woman has her home; people will not waste food and materials, but can exchange with others, talent is used for the public, not necessary just for one's self. Therefore, there is no evil plots and theft, and people are safe even home is open at night. This is the great unity of the world.

22. Communism and Christianity, author: Milton Wan Waiyiu(温伟耀),

published by Tien Dao Publishing House Ltd., Hong Kong (天道书楼有限公司出版(香港)), Jan. 1979. This book also mentioned the advantages and disadvantages of "Practice Theory" (实践论) and "Contradictions Theory" (矛盾论), practiced in China.

23. Five reasons for the collapse of the Soviet Union, see website:
https://graduate.norwich.edu/resources-mmh/articles-mmh/exploring-5-reasons-for-the-collapse-of-the%20soviet-union/

24. Chinese Economic Reform (中国的改革开放), see website:
https://en.wikipedia.org/wiki/Chinese_economic_reform
https://baike.baidu.com/item/改革开放

25. The story of Zhuge Liang(诸葛亮) arrested Meng Huo (孟获) seven times: In 225 AD, Prime Minister of Shu Han dynasty, Zhuge Liang, attacked and arrested a local leader, Meng Huo, seven times, until Meng Huo finally agreed to obey his ruling. See website:
https://baike.baidu.com/item/七擒孟获/435847#1

26. Mencius (372-289 BC) is a master of Confucianism, during the Warring States Period (战国时期) in China. He is a philosopher, politician, and an educator. In his writing "Under the heart of the sentence" (尽心章句下), he said: The most important one is people; government is next; and the last is the king. See website:
https://baike.baidu.com/item/民为贵%EF%BC%8C 社稷次之%EF%BC%8C 君为轻

Chapter 3 Chinese History

China is one of the four ancient civilized nations in the world. [1] China has close to five thousand years history. In this chapter Chinese history will be introduced in two parts, using Qing dynasty as the dividing point. History before Qing dynasty will provide the background of China, while history after it will help us understand the current China.

I. Chinese history before Qing dynasty [2, 3, 4]

I.1 Huang Di (黄帝) [2, 3] (Di means emperor in Chinese) 2690-2590 BC: About 3000 BC, there were some tribes lived at the middle and downstream area of Yellow River. The first recorded leader was Huang Di. Huang Di united with Yan Di (炎帝) defeated Chiyou, a troublemaker. According to the legend, at this time, people already knew how to build palace, to make vehicle, ship, and color clothes. Huang Di's wife, Leizhu (嫘祖), taught women to raise silkworms, to make silk and silk cloth. One of Huang Di's official, Cangjie (仓颉), created words.

I.2 Shaohao, Zhuanxu, Diku (少昊、颛顼、帝喾) 2590-2333 BC: They were all tribe leaders.

I.3 Yao [2, 3] (尧) 2333-2234 BC: Yao was son of Diku. During Yao's ruling, calendar was created; so was the timing of cultivation. According to the legend, Yao lived a simple life; he was good at dealing issues; he worked with his people and was willing to suffer and endure hardship. When he was old, he noticed that his son was not suitable to be the tribe leader. Later, he found Shun who could be the tribe leader. After some time of observation, he decided to let Shun be the tribe leader. This is abdication. During the time of Yao, there was flooding from the Yellow River. Yao asked Gun (鲧) to tame the flooding. Gun used the method of blockage but failed after tried for 9 years.

I.4 Shun [2, 3] (舜) 2233-2184 BC: Shun had good character and was also capable in handling issues. Shun asked Gun's son, Yu (禹), to tame the flooding. Yu used the method of unblocking. After 13 years trying, Yu solved the flooding problem. Yu worked very hard in taming the flooding. Three times, he passed his home, but he didn't go home. Yu's work of taming the flooding was greatly appreciated and Shun decided to abdicate his leadership to Yu.

I.5 Xia Dynasty (夏朝) [2, 4] 2183-1752 BC: It had 17 kings and total 431 years; including the 40 years of seized the throne by Han Zhuo (寒浞). Because Yu did great job in taming the flooding of Yellow River, people supported his son, Qi (启), to inherit his throne, which ended the abdication practice. Tai Kang (太康) was Qi's son. He was a fatuous king.

One time, he went for hunting for 100 days. Later, he was stopped at north side of Luo River by Hou Yi (后羿), a tribe leader at downstream of Yellow River. Hou Yi helped Tai Kang's brother, Zhong Kang (仲康), to be the king. After Zhong Kang died, Hou Yi became the king himself. Hou Yi enjoyed power and good life. He also liked hunting and he trusted Han Zhuo to manage affairs in the country. But Han Zhuo started to win friends to establish his own power. One time, when Hou Yi returned from hunting, Han Zhuo killed him and became the king. Han Zhuo also killed Xiang (相), son of Zhong Kang, but Xiang's wife escaped. Xiang's wife was pregnant. Later, she gave birth to Shao Kang (少康). After Shao Kang grew up, he gathered the people from his tribe and others to defeated Han Zhuo and took back the thorne. The last king of Xia Dynasty is Jie (桀). Jie was a tyrant. He started many large building projects and palaces and lived luxury life. He was defeated and exiled by Tang (汤).

I.6 Shang Dynasty (商朝) [2, 4] 1751-1111 BC: It had 28 kings and total 640 years. Xie (契) was tribe Shang's ancestor. He worked with Yu to taming the flooding and made some contribution. Later, he was prospered in livestock business and became a strong local power. At end of Xia Dynasty, Tang was tribe Shang's leader. He, with the help from Yi Yin (伊尹), defeated Xia Jie's army at Mingtiao (鸣条) (now Fengqui (county) east, Henan (Province)); Jie was exiled to Nanchao (南巢) (today at Chao, Anhui). Tang first stayed at Hao (亳) (now Shangqui, Henan) as his capital. The next 300 years, the capital was moved 5 times, due to internal power struggle and the flooding of Yellow River. The 10th king of Shang Dynasty, was Pan Geng (盘庚). He was a capable man. He moved capital to Yin (殷) (now Anyang northwest, Henan). He organized the nation and stabilized the society. In 20th century, archaeologist found over 100 thousand turtle shells and animal bones at Anyang, with hard to read carved words. After studying, they found these words were recording of various divination during worship, hunting, or war; due to superstition. These words are called oracle bone scripts (甲骨文). There were bronze utensils during Xia Dynasty. Dring Shang Dynasty, the skill of making bronze utensil was further improved. In 1939 AD, a large heavy Shang Dynasty bronze tripod with beautiful patterns was found at Anyang. It is called "Simuwu ding" (司母戊鼎). It weights 875 kg, 133 cm height, 110 cm long, and 79 cm width. Shang Dynasty's last emperor was Zhou (纣). He had military talent. He defeated Dongyi (东夷) at the east and brought the culture of Shang into Huaihe River and Yangtze River basins. But Zhou, like Jie, didn't care people, but himself. He built a large palace at the 2nd capital, Zhaoge (朝歌) (now Qi, Henan). He used Cruel punishment to anyone against him. He was defeated by Wu Wang (武王) of West Zhou.

I.7 West Zhou (西周) [2, 4] 1111-771 BC: It had 12 kings and total 340 years; including 14 years' ministers ruling. Zhou's ancestor belonged to an old tribe. At first, they lived around today's Shaanxi (陕西) and Gansu (甘肃) area. Later, they moved to the field at south of Qishan (岐山) (now Qishan northeast, Shaanxi). During Shang Zhou, Zhou tribe's leader was Ji Chang (姬昌) (Zhou Wen Wang (周文王) ['王' means 'king' in Chinese.]). He took good care of his people, prohibited people to drink wine, and nobles to hunt. His tribe became stronger and stronger. With the help of Jiang Shang (姜尚) (Jiang Taigong (姜太公)), who knew the art of war, he expanded his territory and became even stronger. Later, he moved to Feng (丰) (now Xian southwest, Shaanxi). He died, before he had a chance to fight against Shang Zhou. His son, Wu Wang (武王), became the king. Wu Wang continued using Jiang Taigong as his advisor and using his brother Zhou Gong Dan (周公旦) and Shao Gong Shi (召公奭) as his assistants. Later, Wu Wang used his army of 50 thousand soldiers defeated Zhou's army of 700 thousand soldiers at Muye (牧野) (35 km from Zhaoge). [5] Zhou retreated to Zhouge, committed suicide by burning himself. Wu Wang let Zhou's son, Wu Geng (武庚), as the ruler of Shang's tribe, but at the meantime, he sent his three brothers, Guan Shu (管叔), Cai Shu (蔡叔), and Huo Shu (霍叔), to keep an eye on Wu Geng. Wu Wang also moved capital to Gao Jing (镐京) at east bank of Fenghe (沣河).

Two years later, Wu Wang passed away. His son, Cheng Wang (成王), only 13 years old, became the king. His uncle, Zhou Gong Dan, helped him to manage the country. Guan Shu, Cai Shu, and Huo Shu were not happy about Zhou Gong's new gained power. They united Wu Geng and Dongyi to rebel against the court. With Shao Gong Shi's agreement, Zhou Gong and Jiang Taigong led army to fight the rebellion. After 3 years fighting, they defeated the rebellion; Guan Shu committed suicide, Cai Shu was removed from his office, and Huo Shu was punished to be a soldier. Zhou Gong moved many nobles of Shang's tribe to Luo Yi (洛邑) (now Luoyang City, Henan).

While Zhou Gong helped Cheng Wang managing the nation, he set up a system for the government. 7 years later, he returned the power to Cheng Wang. Cheng Wang's son was Kang Wang (康王). During the ruling of Cheng Wang and Kang Wang, the nation was peaceful. The kings after them used heavy tax and punishment on people. Besides these, there were wars broke out, causing the instability in the society. During Zhou Mu Wang's (周穆王) time, there were 3000 laws to punish people. Criminals were facing 5 kinds of punishment. Zhou Li Wang (周厉王) allowed royal family having special rights on their property, disallowed people's right to use lake or river for living. He also arrested anyone criticizing his ruling. His tyranny finally caused riots of people against him. In 841 BC, people uprose against him. They attacked palace and Li Wang run away to Zhi (彘) (now Huo, Shanxi). Nation was running by Shao Gong Hu (召公虎) and another minister. It lasted for 14 years.

14 years after the ministers ruling, Li Wang died. Ministers supported Prince Jing (靖) as the king. This was Zhou Xuan Wang (周宣王). At this time, Zhou Dynasty was no longer strong anymore. After Xuan Wang, his son, You Wang (幽王), became the king. He didn't like to deal with nation's affairs, but he liked beautiful women. He loved Bao Si (褒姒) very much, but she didn't like to smile. Li Wang gave an order; anyone who could make Bao Si laugh would be rewarded 1000 ounces of gold. Yan Shifu (虢石父), suggested to light up the fire at beacon towers, so that nearby noble kings would lead their army come to protect the capital; when Bao Si saw it, she would laugh. You Wang accepted the suggestion and did it and this really made Bao Si laughed. But lighting fire at beacon towers were for emergency protection of the capital, it should not be used for fun. Later, You Wang deposed the queen and the crowned prince, and set Bao Si as the queen and her son, Bo Fu (伯服), as the crowned prince. The queen's father united Xirong (西戎) to attack Gao Jing. You Wang lighted the fire at beacon towers, but no one came to help him. The army of Xirong entered Gao Jing. They killed You Wang and Bo Fu; took away Bao Si, the treasures, and burnt down Gao Jing. When noble kings knew the attack of Xirong at Gao Jing, they united to fight and chased Xirong away. The original crowned prince became the king, which was Zhou Ping Wang (周平王). When the army of the noble kings left, Xirong came back to attack again. In 770 BC, Ping Wang moved capital to Luo Yi, started the Eastern Zhou. At this time, Zhou dynasty's power was reduced, equivalent to the power of a middle level noble king.

I.8 East Zhou (东周) [2, 4] 770-256 BC: It had 23 kings, total 515 years. In history, this period is further divided to two periods: Spring and Autumn (春秋) and Warring States (战国).

I.8.1 Spring and Autumn Period (春秋时期) 770-475 BC. During this period, China already had tools made of iron and used cow to do the farming. In order to gain territory, noble kings were fighting with each other. The winner became the hegemon and ruled over other noble kings. **The five hegemons during Spring and Autumn** (春秋五霸) The first hegemon was the king of Qi (齐国), now at Shandong Province, the manor of Jiang Taigong. In 686 BC, civil war broke out in Qi. King Qi Xiang-gong (齐襄公) was killed. His two brothers were away from the country at that time. Prince Jiu (公子纠) was at Lu (鲁国) and Prince Xiaobai (公子小白) was at Ju (莒国). Prince Jiu's advisor was Guan Zhong (管仲). Prince Xiaobai's advisor was Bao Shuya (鲍叔牙). When they heard king was killed, both of them hurriedly planned to go back to sieze the throne. Lu Zhuanggong (鲁庄公) decided to escort Prince Jiu back to Qi by himself. Guan Zhong talked to Lu Zhuanggong, Ju is very close to Qi, let me to intercept Prince Xiaobai to prevent him return to Qi first. It was just as Guan Zhong's prediction. On the way to Qi, Guan Zhong met Prince Xiaobai. Guan Zhong shot an arrow at Prince Xiaobai. Prince Xiaobai shout and fell down inside his car. Guan Zhong thought Prince Xiaobai was dead, so he left. In fact, Prince Xiaobai didn't die. The arrow hit the metal part of his clothes and he was pretend to be dead. Prince Xiaobai went back first and became the king of Qi. He was the Qi Huangong (齐桓公).

After Qi Huangong became the king, he defeated Lu and asked Lu to kill Prince Jiu and to send Quan Zong back to Qi. Lu did what was asked to do. After Quan Zong arrived at Qi, Bao Shuya suggested to use him as an important official, because of his talent. At the beginning, Qi Huangong disagreed the suggestion. Later, he changed his mind and use Guan Zong to manage the nation's affairs. Guan Zong developed iron ore, used sea water to make salt, and developed fisheries. Pretty soon, Qi became a rich and strong country. Guan Zong suggested Qi Huangong to respect the emperor of Zhou Dynasty and made justice among the noble kings. Guan Zong helped Qi Huangong to become the hegemon among the noble kings. In 645 BC, Guan Zong died. Two years later, Qi Huangong also died. Qi Huangong's sons fought for the throne and Qi was no longer the hegemon anymore.

Other hegemons of this period were Song Xianggong (宋襄公), Jin Wengong (晋文公), Qin Mugong (秦穆公), and Chu Zhuangwang (楚庄王). They were called the five hegemons of the Spring and Autumn.

Meeting of stop fighting (弭兵会议) [6] When a noble king expanded his territory after fighting, he usually would give some land to his officials. Therefore, the power of some officials increased. They fought each other. Many people hoped this kind of fighting could be stopped. There was an official in Song (宋国), Xiang Shu (向戌). He was busy running back and forth between the country of Jin (晋国) and Chu (楚国), helping the negotiation of cease fire. In 546 BC, Xiang Shu invited Jin, Chu, and several other countries to have a 2nd cease fighting meeting in Song. They signed a covenant, agreed to give tribute to Jin and Chu, except Qin and Qi. This covenant made Jin and Chu to share the power as a hegemon and helped to have a peaceful society for over 50 years.

Wu and Yue (吴国和越国) Wu (吴) was at today's Jiangsu Province (江苏) and Yue (越) was at today's Zhejiang Province (浙江). During late Spring and Autumn Period, Wu Wang (吴王) Helu (阖闾), used Wu Zixu (伍子胥) from Chu as his Prime Minister and Sun Wu (孙武) [7] from Qi as his General. His country became very strong. In 506 BC, his army of 60 thousand soldiers defeated Chu and he became the hegemon. In 496 BC, Yue Wang (越王) Goujian (勾践) became the king of Yue. Helu attacked Yue but was defeated at Zuili (檇李) (now Jiaxing southwest, Zhejiang). Helu was wounded and died later. Helu's son Fuchai (夫差) became the king. Before Helu died, he asked his son to revenge for him. Fuchai asked his men to remind him about this revenge every morning. Two years later, Fuchai defeated Yue. Goujian asked for peace and Fuchai agreed, not to kill Goujian, but he asked Goujian to feed his horses. Two years later, Fuchai released Goujian to return to his home. Goujian obeyed Fuchai on everything, but in fact, he was prepared to revenge. Goujian also sent a beautiful girl, Xi Shi (西施) as a spy to Fuchai, but Fuchai didn't notice the plot. He even killed the prime minister, Wu Zixu, when he warned Fuchai about the plot. In 482 BC, Fuchai went north to fight Qi. When he won the war and came back, he was defeated by Goujian's army. Fuchai asked for peace. Few years later, Goujian attacked Wu again, perished it and killed Fuchai.

Hundred schools of thought (诸子百家) [8] During Spring and Autumn Period and Warring States Period, Eastern Zhou Dynasty was weak, noble kings were fighting with each other, nation's officials gained power, and the society was unstable. Therefore, many people made suggestion about what should be done. This was the period of contending of many philosophers. It made big influence in the future politics and thought in China.

Confucius (孔子) His name is Kong Qio (孔丘); a native of Lu, from 551 to 479 BC. He was the founder of Confucianism. His father was a low rank military officer. When he was 3 years old, his father passed away. His mother brought him to Qufu (曲阜) (now Qufu, Shandong), where he grew up. When he was young, he worked very hard. Zhou Gong Dan was his idol. He was familiar with the old customs. He mastered the 6 arts during his times (etiquette, music, archery, driving, writing, and computing). Before he was 30 years old, he was already well known. At the beginning, he set up school to teach students. Once, Lu Zhaogong (鲁昭公) sent him to Luyi to check the ceremony and music of Zhou Dynasty. When he was 50 years old, Lu Dinggong (鲁定公) assigned a position for him in his court. But soon, he left Lu and started to travel around the world for 7-8 years. He advocated to restore the ritual system (hierarchical system) of Zhou Dynasty, but no king planned to use him. Later, he returned to Lu and started to write and teach. He had 3000 students. Among them, 72 became famous. He advocated benevolence, loyal, forgiveness, moderation, restoration of ritual system, improving personalities, and knowing how to deal issues.

Lao Zi (老子) His name is Li Er (李耳), a native of Chu; from 571 to 471 BC. He was the founder of Taoism. He wrote "Morality" ("道德经"). He thought everything has positive and negative sides.

I.8.2 Warring States Period (战国时期) [2, 4] 475-256 BC. Noble kings fought each other during Spring and Autumn Period. During Warring States Period, only 7 countries left. They were Han (韩), Zhao (赵), Wei (魏), Qi (齐), Chu (楚), Yan (燕), and Qin (秦). At the end, Qin defeated the other 6 countries.

Qin (秦国) At beginning, Qin was a backward nation among the 7. In 361 BC, Qin Xiaogong (秦孝公) became the king. He decided to make Qin a strong nation and he opened his court to the talents. He used Shang Yang (商鞅) from Wei (卫国) as Prime Minister. Shang Yang advocated to develop agriculture, using reward and punishment for motivation. He made Qin very strong. In 350 BC, Shang Yang started his 2nd reform: abolishing the mine field system (井田制), opened the roads in field for cultivation, set up county, county head was appointed by government, practicing centralization, moved capital to Xianyang (咸阳) (now Xianyang northeast, Shaanxi). After 10 years, Qin became a rich and strong nation.

United together against a strong one or unite with a strong one against an enemy (合纵与连横) They were two diplomatic and military strategies used during Warring States Period. The 1st one means united weak countries against the strong one, such as Qin. The 2nd one means united with a strong country to attack the enemy. Su Qin (苏秦) advocated using the 1st strategy against Qin. Zhang Yi (张仪) advocated the 2nd strategy to help Qin. They were classmate, without definite political opinion or intention to serve any country. They did care to have a position in a court.

Su Qin was a native of Luoyi (雒邑) (now Luoyang City east, Henan). At beginning, he planned to serve emperor of Zhou Dynasty, but failed. Therefore, he went to Qin. He proposed a way to defeat the other 6 countries to the new king, Qin Huiwen Wang (秦惠文王), but wasn't accepted. After over one year at Qin, he used up his money and returned home. At home, he was look down by his family. He decided to study the art of war to prepare himself. After more than a year, in 334 BC, he went to Yan. He suggested Yan Wengong (燕文公) to united Zhao to fight against Qin and his suggestion was accepted. Yan Wengong gave him many gifts, vehicles, and horses, asking him to contact Zhao. When Su Qin arrived at Zhao, he encouraged Zhao to united other countries to fight against Qin. Zhao Suhou (赵肃候) agreed with Su Qin's suggestion, giving him one thousand Jin (斤) [about 500 kg] gold, one thousand rolls of silk, 100 vehicles with horses, and 100 pairs of jade for him to work with other noble kings. In 333 BC, six noble kings gathered at Huanshui (洹水) (now at northern Henan), signed a covenant for cooperation. Su Qin was ordained as the leader to overlook the cooperation.

Zhang Yi was a native of Wei. At first, he planned to serve Wei Wang or Chu Wang, but failed. Later, he heard Su Qin became the leader of six countries at Zhao. He went to Su Qin hope to have a job. But Su Qin sent him to Qin and spent lots money to ask Qin Huiwen Wang's (秦惠文王) subordinates to recommend Zhang Yi; to help Zhang Yi gained a position in Qin's court. Huiwen Wang's Prime Minister advocated to attack Zhao, but Zhang Yi let the six countries to suspect each other and broke their cooperation. Huiwen Wang also accepted Zhang Yi's suggestion returned some cities back to Wei, arranged royal marriage relationship with Yan, dissolved cooperation between Qi and Chu. Not long after, Su Qin was murdered, and the cooperation among the six countries disappeared.

In 270 BC, Qin Zhaoxiang Wang (秦昭襄王) met Fan Sui (范雎), a native of Wei. Fan Sui suggested Zhaoxiang Wang to use a strategy to attack closeby country and to make friend with far away countries to conquer the six countries. Few years later, Zhaoxiang Wang used Fan Sui as his Prime Minister and defeated Wei, Han, and Zhao. When Zhaoxiang Wang died, Qin Zhuangxiang Wang (秦庄襄王) became the king. He died three years later. The 13 years old prince, Qin Wang Ying Zheng (秦王嬴政) became the king [Ying Zheng was his last and first name]; prime minister Lu Buwei (吕不韦) helped him to manage the nation. When Ying Zheng was 22 years old, he deposed Lu Buwei's duty and started to deal the nation's affairs by himself. In 227 BC, Yan's prince Dan (丹) arranged the assassin, Jin Ke (荆轲) to kill Ying Zheng, but failed. Ying Zheng sent troops to attack Yan. Yan Wang run away, killed Prince Dan, and asked for peace. At this time, Han was under Qin's control, Zhao only had one city left. Ying Zheng first conquered Wei (225 BC). Then, he conquered Chu, Yan, and Zhao (222 BC). In 221 BC, he attacked Qi. Qi Wang surrendered, and Qin conquered the central plain of China.

Hundred schools of thought (诸子百家) [8] **Mencius** (孟子) His first name is Ke (轲), a native of Zou (邹国), 372-289 BC. He was a master of Confucianism. He advocated: people are the most important ones in a nation, use benevolent policy to rule a nation, and human nature is good. He wrote a book, "Mencius".

Xunzi (旬子) He focused on Confucianism and added the good points of Taoism (道), Legalism (法), Moism (墨), and Mingism (名). He considered human nature is evil.

Zhuangzi (庄子) He was a master of Taoism. He advocated to follow the nature, ruling a nation without disturbance.

Han Feizi (韩非子) He was a master of legalism. He advocated using law to rule a nation, reform, and political power centralization.

Mozi (墨子) He is the founder of Moism. He advocated everyone is equal, love, thrifty, justice, and against aggression.

I.9 Qin Dynasty (秦朝) [2, 4] 221-206 BC: It had 3 kings, total 15 years. Qin Wang Ying Zheng called himself Qin Shihuang (秦始皇) (The 1st Emperor of Qin), after he conquered the six countries. He abolished feudal system and adopted the county system in order to gain power for the central government. He divided nation into 36 counties. He unified the width of vehicle and road, writing words, and measuring systems (length/weight/volume). He fought in the north against Xiongnu (匈奴) [a foreign tribe], recovered the land at Hetao (河套) [a vast land bounded by Yellow River, north of Shannxi Province] and added another county. He also sent 500 thousand soldiers to the south and added 3 counties. Some intellectuals criticized national affairs. He ordered to burn the books of different schools and buried over 460 intellectuals alive.

Bolangsha assassination (博浪沙事件) After Qin Shihuang eliminated the six countries, he moved 120 thousand rich families to the capital Xianyang, to prevent the nobles to rebel against him and for better control of them. He confiscated all the weapons in the nation. He frequently went to places to inspect situation over there. In the spring of 218 BC, Qin Shihuang passed Bolangsha (博浪沙) (now Yuanyang, Henan). Suddenly, a big iron ball flied toward his team. It hit and smashed a deputy's vehicle after his. After searching, they didn't find the assassin. This assassin was a strong man hired by Zhang Liang (张良), a native of Han. After this incident, Zhang Liang fled to Xiapi (下邳) (now Suining northwest, Jiangsu) and hid himself there. At the meantime, he studied the art of war and tried to be back again.

The plot at Shaqiu (沙丘的阴谋) In 210 BC, Qin Shihuang inspected southeastern area. He left in winter and came back in summer. He felt sick, when he arrived Shandong area. Medical treatment didn't help him. At Shaqui (沙丘) (now Guangzhong northwest, Hebei), his illness got worse. He told Zhao Gao (赵高), a close eunuch of his, to tell Price Fusu (扶苏) to go back to Xianyang to arrange the funeral, but before the message was sent out, Qin Shihuang died. Prime Minister Li Si (李斯) suggested not to let public know the death, until they were back to Xianyang. On the road, Zhao Gao persuaded Li Si to send a fake letter from Qin Shihuang, blamed

Fusu didn't work hard, angry at the emperor, and should die. Fusu didn't know this is a fake letter. He killed himself. Zhao Gao set his master, Prince Hu Hai (胡亥), to be the emperor. This was Qin Er Shi (秦二世) (The 2nd Emperor of Qin). Zhao Gao persuaded Qin Er Shi to kill his 12 brothers, 10 sisters, and some high officials. Later, Zhao Gao killed the Li Si, and became the Prime Minister himself.

Riots During the time of Qin Shihuang, China had 20 million people, but 2-3 million were sent to build great wall, defending southern terrriorty, to build palace and royal tombs and other services. People complained their life. In 209 BC, at Yangcheng (阳城) (now Dengfeng southeast, Henan), there were two officers escorted 900 people to Yuyang (渔阳) (now Miyun southwest, Hebei) to guard the place. These two officers selected two people to help control the group. One was Chen Sheng (陈胜), a long-term labor, and the other was Wu Guang (吴广), a peasant. When they arrived at Dazexiang (大泽乡) (now Su southeast, Anhui), the rain was heavy, and they were not able to move forward. They would miss the deadline. According to the law, they were all put to death. Chen Sheng and Wu Guang decided to revolt. They killed the two officers and led people to riot. They didn't have weapon, but they used sticks as their weapon. Quickly, they occupied Daze Township. Many nearby farmers came to support them. Chen Sheng became the king. His nation was called Zhang Chu (张楚). After the uprising of Chen Sheng and Wu Quang, many riots broke out in the nation. Chen Sheng sent troop to help the riots at different places and gained a large territory. Within 3 months, nobles of six countries rose up tried to restore their country. When Chen Sheng's army about reaching Guanzhong (关中) (the area west of Hangu Pass (函谷关)), Qin Er Shi sent General Zhang Han (章邯) to counterattack. The uprising army fought alone, without the help from the nobles of the six countries. They finally were defeated, and Chen Sheng was killed.

Liu Bang and Xiang Yu (刘邦和项羽) Although Chen Sheng died, the force against Qin Dynasty kept growing; especially at south, there was Xiang Liang (项梁) (son of former Chu's General Xiang Yan (项燕)) at Kuaiji County (会稽郡) (now at Zhejiang Province). Xiang Yu (项羽) was Xiang Liang's nephew. They attacked and occupied Kuaiji. Then, they led 8 thousand soldiers conquered many places. They also accepted other riot troops and became a big force.

Liu Bang (刘邦) was a native of Pei County (沛县) (now Pei, Jiangsu). He was a head official of a local township (in charge of 5 km area). He was ordered to bring a group of people to Lishan (骊山) to do hard work, but people continued run away. Later, he led the remaining people to revolt. At the beginning, with the help from Xiao He (萧何), a civil official at Pei County, and Cao Shen (曹参), a prison officer at Pei County, he occupied Pei County. Later, he met Zhang Liang and they decided to follow Xiang Liang.

Xiang Liang organized the uprising army and used Fan Zeng (范增) as his advisor. They set up Chu Wang and defeated Zhang Han. At this moment, Xiang Liang relaxed his vigilance and he was killed under Zhang Han's counterattack. Then, Zhang Han went north to attack Zhao. Zhao Wang was trapped at Julu (巨鹿) and he asked Chu Wang for help. Chu Wang sent Song Yi (宋义) led 200 thousand soldiers to rescue Zhao Wang; Xiang Yu was the vice commander. Chu Wang also sent Liu Bang to attack Xianyang. When Song Yi arrived at the front, for 46 days, he didn't attack the enemy, but tried to keep his force intact. Later, Xiang Yu killed Song Yi and reported his action to Chu Wang. Chu Wang had no choice, but to let him be the commander. Xiang Yu sent 20 thousand soldiers to cut off the food supply of Qin's army. Then, he sent his main force across the river to attack the enemy. He gave his soldiers 3 days food and sank all the ships in the river. His men fought fiercely and defeated Qin's army. Finally, the siege at Julu was relieved. Zhang Han asked Qin Wang for help, but he didn't get any help. He surrendered to Xiang Yu.

Liu Bang advanced toward Xianyang smoothly. Pretty soon, his army arrived Xianyang. Zhao Gao knew the end was coming. Zhao Gao killed Qin Er Shi and set his nephew, Ziying (子婴) as the emperor. Ziying killed Zhao Gao, but he surrendered to Liu Bang and ended the Qin Dynasty. When Liu Bang entered Xianyang, he accepted the suggestion from Zhang Liang and Fan Kuai (樊哙). He sealed the warehouses, abolished Qin's law, and set up three rules for people to obey: 1) Killing people would die, 2) Hurt people would be punished, 3) stealing or robbing would be punished. People liked his ruling and he won the heart of the people in Guanzhong.

The banquet at Hongmen (鸿门宴) After Xiang Yu accepted Zhang Han's surrender, he had problems controlling the Qin soldiers of over 200 thousand and he finally killed them by burying them alive in a big pit. This showed the cruel side of Xiang Yu. Later, he also went to Xianyang, camped at Hongmen (鸿门) (now Lintong northeast, Shaanxi). He had 400 thousand soldiers and Liu Bang had 100 thousand soldiers. Xiang Yu's advisor, Fan Zeng, suggested to kill Liu Bang to avoid future troubles. In the morning of the next day, Liu Bang came to visit Xiang Yu to explain that he was not against Xiang Yu. This made Xiang Yu happy and he invited Liu Bang for dinner. At dinner, Fan Zeng hinted Xiang Yu to kill Liu Bang, but Xiang Yu didn't do anything and let Liu Bang return safely to his camp. This was the banquet at Hongmen.

When Xiang Yu arrived at Xianyang, he killed Ziying and over 800 Qin's nobles. He burnt Epang Palace (阿房宫) and it was burnt for 3 months. When Xiang Yu was in power, he changed Chu Wang's name to Yi Di (义帝). He set up 18 noble kings to award his generals and the nobles of the six countries. He named himself Overlord of the West Chu (西楚霸王). It meant he was above all the noble kings in the kingdom of West Chu. Every noble king had his assigned territory. Then, Xiang Yu returned to his capital, Pengcheng (彭城) (now Xuzhou, Jiangsu). Liu Bang was named Han Wang (汉王). His territory was at Bashu (巴蜀) and Hanzhong (汉中). Liu Bang went to his territory and lived at Nan Zheng (南郑) (now Hanzhong east, Shaanxi). He used Xiao He as his prime minister. Xiao He met Han Xin (韩信) and recognized Han Xin's rare talent. Xiao He recommended Han Xin to Liu Bang and Han Xin was named the Chief Commander (大将军) of his army.

Fighting between Chu and Han (楚汉相争) In August, 206 BC, Liu Bang and Han Xin attacked Zhang Han at Guanzhong. Less than 3 months, they conquered Guanzhong. At this moment, Qi was in turmoil. Xiang Yu decided to calm the turmoil in Qi first. But Liu Bang continued moving eastward. When he conquered Pengcheng, Xiang Yu came back, and they fought at Pengcheng. Liu Bang was defeated badly. His father and wife (Lu Zhi) were captured. Liu Bang retreated to Xingyang (荥阳) and Chenggao (成皋) (now Xingyang, Henan). He used tricks to let Fan Zeng left Xiang Yu. Two years later, Xiang Yu decided to attacked Peng Yue (彭越) at the east. He told Cao Jiu (曹咎) to stay at Chenggao and not to fight with Liu Bang. Everyday, Liu Bang scolded at Cao Jiu across the bank of Sishui (汜水). Cao Jiu could not bear the scold. He sent his men across the river to attack Liu Bang. He was defeated badly and committed suicide. When Xiang Yu returned, two armies fought again. At this time, Xiang Yu needed some food supply and Liu Bang needed more troops. Liu Bang asked for peace, asking the return of his father and wife, and using Honggou (鸿沟) [canal] as their boundary. Xiang Yu agreed. Less than two months, Liu Bang contacted Han Xin, Peng Yue, and Ying Bu (英布) to attack Xiang Yu together. They defeated Xiang Yu. At first, Xiang Yu was trapped at Gaixia (垓下) (now Lingbi southeast, Anhui). Later, he committed suicide at Wujiang (乌江) (now He northeast, Anhui).

I.10 Han Dynasty (汉朝) [2, 4] It can be divided into 3 periods: West Han, Xin, and East Han.

I.10.1 West Han (西汉) 206 BC-8 AD: It had 11 kings, total 214 years.

Xiongnu (匈奴) In 202 BC, Liu Bang defeated Xiang Yu and became the emperor, Han Gao Zu (汉高祖). He was the 1st person to become an emperor as an ordinary people in Chinese history. Empress Lu killed Han Xin and Peng Yue. Later, Ying Bu rebelled and was killed also. At this time, Xiongnu Empire rose up at Mongolia. Its leader, Modu Chanyu (冒顿单于), led a troop with 400 thousand soldiers to attack China. They besieged Jingyang (晋阳) (now Taiyuan, Shanxi). In the winter of 200 BC, Gao Zu led army, went to Jingyang to relieve its siege. He won few battles and freed Jingyang. He sent people to check the situation of Xiongnu. The report was Xiongnu's army were weak, soldiers were either old men or weak people. He checked several times, but the results were the same. Liu Jing (刘敬), Gao Zu's advisor, warned Gao Zu that Xiongnu's army was hiding, but Gao Zu didn't believe. He continued to fight Xiongnu. When he arrived at Pi Cheng (平城) (now Datong northeast, Shanxi), suddenly, Xiongnu's regular army appeared. Gao Zu was trapped on Bai Deng Mountain (白登山) for 7 days. Later, counselor Chen Ping (陈平) used gold and jewelry to bribe Chanyu's wife to persuade Chanyu to retreat and helped Liu Bang to escape back to Changan (长安) (now Xian, Shaanxi). From this incident on, Gao Zu using Liu Jing's suggestion using monarch marriage to make peace with Xiongnu.

White horse covenant When Gao Zu was seriously ill at his old age, he summoned his high officials. In front of them, he killed a white horse, he asked his officials to use its blood to make a covenant; swearing only a person with last name 'Liu' could be noble king, anyone violated this rule, people should be united together to attack him. [9] His officials did this swear and Gao Zu was happy. This was the white horse covenant.

Ruling with Huang Lao practice (黄老之治) [Rule a nation with the practice of Huang Di and Lao Zhi; a popular Taoism practice in ancient China.] In 195 BC, Gao Zhu died. Prince Liu Ying (刘盈) became the emperor; Han Hui Di (汉惠帝). Next year, Hui Di went to visit the Prime Minister Xiao He, who was seriously ill. He asked Xiao He whether he should use Cao Shen as his Prime Minister. Xiao He agreed his choice. In the past, when Gao Zhu made his eldest son, Liu Fei (刘肥), as the noble king of Qi, he made Cao Shen to be the Prime Minister of Qi to help Liu Fei. Cao Shen was a General, when he arrived Qi, he asked local people how to rule the place. Later, he met a hermit, Gai Gong (盖公) and used his suggestion to rule the place using Huang Lao practice: Ruling people without disturbance and let people have a peaceful life. Cao Shen was the Prime Minister of Qi for 9 years and Qi was very stable. When Xiao He died, Hui Di asked Cao Shen to come to the capital to be his Prime Minister. Cao Shen still using Huang Lao practice to rule the country.

Empress Lu seized the power When Hui Di was the emperor, the power of the nation was gradually fell into the hand of his mother, Empress Dowager Lu. When Hui Di died, Empress Dowager Lu set an infant to be the emperor and she was in power. In order to solidify her power, she named many her relative with surname 'Lu' as noble kings, ignored the white horse covenant. High officials were angry, but no one dared to say anything. At the 8th year of Empress Dowager's ruling, she was seriously ill. Before she died, she named Lu Chan (吕产) as the Prime Minister, leading the North Army, and Lu Lu (吕禄) as the Commander-in-chief, leading the South Army. Li Ji (郦寄) is the son of a high official Li Shang (郦商). He was a close friend of Lu Lu. He persuaded Lu Lu to give the army's power to Grand Commandant (太尉) Zhou Bo (周勃) to avoid the suspicion of high officials. Lu Lu agreed. This ended the power of the family of Lu in the court. After this event, high officials supported Dai Wang (代王) Liu Huan (刘桓) as the emperor, Han Wen Di (汉文帝). Wen Di was Gao Zhu's grandson; a person with good characters. He abolished the law that punishing a whole family, if one of the family committed crime.

Ti Ying saved her father (缇萦) During the time of Wen Di, at Linzi (临淄) (now Linbo, Shandong), there was an intellectual, named Chunyu Yi (淳于意). He liked medical science. He frequently treated patients and became a well-known doctor. Later, he became an official in charge of granary (太仓令). But he was not good at flattering and dealing with people, so he resigned and went to be a doctor. One day, he treated a rich merchant's wife, but she died few days later. Ther merchant sued hime and he was put in jail. He was sentenced to have corporal punishment (to have tattoo on face, cut off nose, or cut off a leg). Chunyu Yi had 5 daughters, but no son to take the punishment for him. When he was escorted to Changan for the punishment, his youngest daughter, Ti Ying, went with him. She planned to take the punishment for her father. She asked someone to write a request to the emperor, saying the corporal punishment was too cruel, she's willing to be a servant to exchange for her father's punishment. When Wen Di saw the request, he was touched and had passion for Ti Ying. He discussed this issue with his officials and decided to replace the corporal punishment to spank.

The chaos of the seven noble kings After Wen Di, Jing Di (景帝) Liu Qi (刘启) became the emperor. At this time, in addition to the county system, the nation also set up 22 noble kings. Some noble king was powerful, just like a ruler of an independent country. Jing Di used Chao Cuo (晁错) as his Vice Prime Minister (御史大夫). Chao Cuo suggested Jing Di to reduce the land of noble kings and their power. When they were still discussing this issue, Wu Wang (吳王) Liu Bi (刘濞) rebelled. He also persuaded 6 other noble kings to rebel. Jing Di sent Grand Commandant Zhou Yafu (周亚夫) to fight the rebels. Someone suggested to kill Chao Cuo to quiet the rebel. So did Jing Di, but rebellion continued, because some noble kings planned to rebel long time ago. Fortunately, Zhou Yafu was a capable general; within 3 months, the rebellion was perished.

Lured the enemy at Mayi (马邑诱敌) After 60 years of Huang Lao practice during Wen Di and Jing Di, Han Dynasty became very rich and strong, but Xiongnu at north still was the big problem. After Jing Di, Han Wu Di (汉武帝) Liu Che (刘彻) became the emperor. In 135 BC, Junchen Chanyu (军臣单于) of Xiongnu requested monarch marriage to Han Dynasty. General Wang Hui (王恢) advocated to fight with Xiongnu, but most officials were against fighting. Therefore, Wu Di granted to have monarch marriage with Xiongnu.

Two years later, a big merchant at Mayi, Nie Yi (聂壹), suggested to lure Xiongnu to Mayi and ambushed them. Wu Di agreed and sent 300 thousand soldiers to Mayi. Nie Yi lured Xiongnu to Mayi. He killed few criminals and told Xiongnu that he already killed the county head of Mayi. Therefore, Junchen Chanyu led 100 thousand men to loot Mayi. But on his way, he captured a village head and learned the plot. He run away. From this time on, no monarch marriage was mentioned anymore, but war.

Fightings with Xiongnu In 129 BC, Xiongnu came to attack China. Wu Di sent Wei Qing (卫青), Li Guang (李广), etc. four generals to fight Xiongnu. Among them, General Li Guang was the eldest. During Wen Di's time, he was already a general. Xiongnu were afraid of him, calling him "flying general (飞将军)", because his presence was hard to predict and his archery was very good. During this war, Xiongnu sent large troop to fight against Li Guang and ordered to capture Li Guang alive. During the war, Li Guang was wounded and captured. He was put on a hammock between two horses. On the road, he seized a nice horse and run back to his camp. Although he came back, he was sentenced to die, because of losing the war. Fortunately, according to the Han law, people could use money to buy back his life. This helped Li Guang to be alive.

There were two other generals, Wei Qing and Huo Qubing (霍去病). They made great accomplishments during their fight with Xiongnu. Wei Qing was a servant at Cao minister's home, a very humble position. Later, his sister, Wei Zifu (卫子夫) became Wu Di's favored wife and he was also put in high position. In 124 BC, Wei Qing led 100 thousand cavalrymen to attack the Right Xianwang (右贤王) of Xiongnu [2nd leader]. One night, his troop did a rapid march of 600-700 li (里) [about 250-291 km; 1li=

415.8 m]. They defeated the Right Xianwang, captured over 10 small kings and over 15 thousand men. This was a big victory. Right away, Wu Di commanded Wei Qing to be the Commander-in-chief (大将军). Next year, Xiongnu came to attack again. Wu Di commanded Wei Qing with 6 other generals and large army to fight. Wei Qing's nephew [on his mother side], Huo Qubing, only 18 years old went with him. Wei Qing sent 4 groups to attack Xiongnu. At night, 3 groups came back, without finding the main force of Xiongnu. Huo Qubing led 800 men, walking few hundred li and encountered Xiongnu's camp. He entered the largest tent, killed one leader and captured 2 others. His troop killed over two thousand men. Then, they returned to their camp. Wei Qing was worried about Huo Qubing, but glad to see his return. They found out the leader they killed was a Xiongnu head at grandfather level and the 2 captives were Chanyu's uncle and Prime Minister. Huo Qubing made a big accomplishment.

In 121 BC, Wu Di commanded Huo Qubing led 10 thousand cavalrymen, from Longxi (陇西) (now Gansu west) to attack Xiongnu. He fought 6 days, Xiongnu retreated. He marched forward about over 1000 li [416 km], reached the vassal state of Xiongnu. In order to eliminate the Xiongnu's invasion, in 119 BC, Wu Di commanded Wei Qing and Huo Qubing, each led 50 thousand best troops to attack Xiongnu. Wei Qing, across the desert, marched over 1000 li, defeated Yizhixie Chanyu (伊穉邪单于) of Xiongnu and chased him to Zhiyanshan (寘颜山) (now Mongolian plateau Hangai Mountain south). Huo Qubing also across the desert, marched over 2000 li [832 km], defeated Left Xianwang (左贤王), all the way to Langjuxushan (狼居胥山). 70-80 thousand of Xiongnu's main force was eliminated. From this time on, south of the desert, no more Xiongnu existed.

Banned all schools, except Confucianism Wu Di used Dong Zhongshu's (董仲舒) suggestion, banned all schools, except Confucianism. This action let Confucianism become the traditional school in China and made big influence in China.

Zhang Qian (张骞) **visited Xiyu** (西域, the west) Wu Di was hoping to unite the defeated Yueshigao (月氏国) to fight Xiongnu together. Therefore, he sent people to Xiyu to accomplish this task. Zhang Qian volunteered for this job. In 139 BC, he led a team of over 100 men to Xiyu to find Yueshigao. After few days' travel, he was detained by Xiongnu. He escaped after detained more than 10 years. He went to Dawan (大宛). The king of Dawan was nice to him and escorted him to Yueshigao. But the ruler of Yueshigao had no intention to fight against Xiongnu anymore, because they settled down at an area near Daxia (now northern Afghan) and established a nation, named Big Yueshigao. Zhang Qian stayed more than one year and also visited Daxia. Then, he left for home. On his way home, he was detained again by Xiongnu. Fortunately, civil war broke out in Xiongnu. He escaped and returned to Changan after staying 13 years at Xiyu. In 119 BC, Xiongnu was defeated by Han Dynasty. Wu Di sent Zhang Qian to Xiyu again with 300 men and gifts for a friendly visit.

The achievements of Wu Di Wu Di became an emperor, when he was 16 years old. He reined 54 years, 141-87 BC. He was the 7th emperor in Han Dynasty. His achievements were: defeated Xiongnu, expanded territory, communicated with the nations in Xiyu, banned all schools except Confucianism, practiced "push grace" order, unified currency, nationalization of salt and iron, etc. At his old age, he advocated farming, no more war. [10]

Shiji (史记) **by Sima Qian** (司马迁) In 99 BC, during Wu Di's time, history official (太史令) Sima Qian said few nice words for General Li Ling (李陵), who surrendered to Xiongnu under a bad situation and was put in jail. Because he didn't have money, he also suffered the castration punishment (宫刑). [11] He wrote "Shiji" (The Records of the Grand Historian), recorded history from Huang Di to Han Wu Di. It has 130 chapters, total 520 thousand words. It is a great precious historical writing.

Su Wu the shepherd (苏武牧羊) In 100 BC, Wu Di sent Su Wu to visit Xiongnu. He was 40 years old. Some issue happened and Su Wu was detained by Xiongnu. They sent him to North Sea (now Lake Baikal) to be a shepherd. 19 years later, he was released and returned home.

Wu Di's eldest son was framed by an official and committed suicide. After Wu Di died, his 8 years old son became the emperor, Han Zhao Di (汉昭帝). Commander-in-chef Huo Guang (霍光) helped him managing the nation. Zhao Di died, when he was 21 years old. He had no son. Huo Guang selected Wu Di's grandson, Changyi Wang (昌邑王) Liu He (刘贺) to be the emperor. After 27 days, they found Liu He did many bad things and he only knew to have fun. High officials in the court decided to replace him. They selected Wu Di's great grandson, Liu Xun (刘询), to be the emperor, Han Huan Di (汉宣帝). During Huan Di's time, Xiongnu had internal power struggle problem and was divided into 5 groups. They fought each other and became weaker. Among them, Huhanxie Chanyu (呼韩邪单于) came to Changan to visit Huan Di, asking help. He was the first Xiongnu leader came to visit China's emperor. Huan Di agreed to help him. Because of this, many countries at Xiyu (西域, the west) established relationship with Han Dynasty. After Huan Di died, his son, Han Yuan Di (汉元帝), became the emperor. Few years later, Zhizhi Chanyu (郅支单于) of Xiongnu invaded the countries in Xiyu, also killed Han's diplomatic envoys. Han united with the countries in Xiyu defeated Xiongnu and killed Zhizhi Chanyu. In 33 BC, Huhanxie Chanyu came to Changan the 2nd time, asking to establish monarch marriage. Yuan Di gave the beautiful lady, Wang Zhaojun (王昭君), to be his wife. Wang Zhaojun was popular and welcomed by the people of Xiongnu. Almost 60 years, there was no fighting between Xiongnu and Han Dynasty.

After Yuan Di died, his son Han Cheng Di (汉成帝) became the emperor. Cheng Di was dissolute and incompetent. Power of the nation fell into the hand of his mother, Empress Dowager Wang Zhengjun (王政君). She named 7 of her brothers to be the high officials. Among them, the eldest, Wang Feng (王凤), became the Grand General. [13] Brothers and nephews of Empress Dowager Wang were proud and luxury, except her nephew, Wang Mang (王莽), who was humble and thrift. Later, Wang Mang also became a high military official. After Cheng Di died, less than 10 years, Han had two emperors – Ai Di (哀帝) and Ping Di (平帝). When Ping Di became the emperor, he was 12 years old. Wang Mang helped him for nation's affairs. Two years later, Wang Mang killed Ping Di by poison. He set a two-years old baby Ruziying (孺子婴) as the emperor and he himself became the substituted emperor. In January, 9 AD, Wang Mang usurped the throne.

I.10.2 Xin (新) 9-23 AD: It had 1 king, total 15 years. When Wang Mang became the emperor, he implemented three retro policies: 1) All the land in the nation belonged to the emperor, not allowed to sell or buy. 2) Servant was private own, not allowed to sell or buy. 3) Assess goods price and currency reform. The first two was opposed by nobles and richs. The third one became a tool of bribery. No one supported these policies. Three years later, he abolished the first two policies. Wang Mang recruited people for labors, increased tax, indulging cruel officials, all made people in hardship.

Green Forest Army (绿林军) In 17 AD, there were famine at Jingzhou (荆州) (now Hubei central south). Wang Kuang (王匡) led 7-8 thousand famine refugees occupied the Lulingshan (绿林山, Green Forest Mountain) (now Dahongshan, Hubei). Wang Mang sent 20 thousand soldiers to calm the riot, but they were defeated and lost few cities. The Green Forest Army (GFA) was increased to over 50 thousand people.

Red Eyebrow Army (赤眉军) In 18 AD, Fan Chong (樊崇) led few hundred men at Juxian (莒县) conquered Taishan (泰山). In less than one year, they had over 10 thousand people. In 22 AD, Wang Mang sent Wang Kuang (王匡) (not the one from GFA) and Lian Dan (廉丹) led 100 thousand soldiers to calm the rebel. For the easy of recognization, Fan Chong told his men to put red color on their eyebrow. This was the Red Eyebrow Army (REA). REA was strict in discipline, not allowed to bother people. They were much welcomed by people. They defeated Wang Mang's army, killed half of its soldiers. At the meantime, REA expanded to over 100 thousand men.

Emperor Gengshi (更始皇帝) At Chongling Village (舂陵乡), Nanyang County (南阳郡) (now Ningyuan north, Hunan), there were two brothers, Liu Yan (刘縯) and Liu Xiu (刘秀) led 7-8 thousand people uprising. They joined the GFA and had over 100 thousand people. They attacked Wang Mang, won few battles, and became a big force. In 22 AD, they supported a fading noble, Liu Xuan (刘玄), as their king, Emperor Gengshi, and called their arm, Army of Han. In 23 AD, they conquered Kunyang (昆阳) (now Ye, Henan), Yancheng (郾城) (now Yancheng, Henan), and Dingling (定陵) (now Yancheng northwest, Henan). Wang Mang sent 430 thousand soldiers to attack Kunyang, but was defeated, only few thousand escaped. Later, Han army attacked Changan, destroyed Wang Mang.

I.10.3 East Han (东汉) 25-220 AD: It had 13 kings, total 196 years. After the battle of Kunyang, the prestige of Liu Yan and Liu Xiu was greatly increased. Emperor Gengshi used an excuse that Liu Yan disobeyed order and killed Liu Yan. He sent Liu Xiu to an area north of Yellow River to do appeasing work. Liu Xiu used this opportunity to expand his own territory. He conquered Hebei. In 25 AD, at Hao (鄗) (now Baixiang north, Hebei), Liu Xiu became the king, Han Guangwu Di (汉光武帝), started the Dynasty of East Han.

Emperor Gengshi first set the capital at Luoyang (洛阳). Then, he moved the capital to Changan. He was corrupted, didn't work on nation's affairs, but spent time on enjoyment. The REA of 200 thousand men came to attack Changan and won few battles. Wang Kuang and several other generals of GFA surrendered to REA. Very soon, REA took Changan.

REA made a 15 years old youth who attended cow, Liu Penzi (刘盆子) as their king. At Changan, REA didn't have enough food, so they went westward, but that didn't solve their problem. At the meantime, Guangwu Di took Luoyang and started to fight REA. In January, 27 AD, he wiped out REA. Then, he eliminated two strong leaders at Longyou (陇右) (now Gansu) and Shudi (蜀地) (now Sichuan) and united China. He set Luoyang as the capital.

After Guangwu Di became the emperor, he asked Ban Biao (班彪) to sort out the history of West Han Dynasty. Ban Biao had two sons, Ban Gu (班固) and Ban Chao (班超). When Guangwu Di died, Han Ming Di (汉明帝) became the emperor. He asked Ban Gu to continue his father's work, writing "Han Shu" (汉书) (The Book of Han Dynasty), and Ban Chao to copy the writing. Ban Chao didn't like the writing job. He decided to join the army to fight against Xiongnu. In 73 AD, Ban Chao followed the Commander-in-chef Dou Gu (窦固) to fight against Xiongnu. Dou Gu sent him to contact with the Shanshanguo (鄯善国) in Xiyu (西域, the west). After some efforts, he accomplished this assignment. Later, Ming Di asked him to contact with the Yutianguo (于阗国). He also did it. These two countries were big nations in Xiyu. Countries in Xiyu lost contact with Han for almost 65 years. Now, they were connected again.

East Han after the 4th emperor, Han He Di (汉和帝), all the emperors were young kids. They needed Empress Dowager, their mother, to help manage the nation. Empress Dowager often would use her relatives for help. Therefore, power fell into the hand of royal relatives. When the emperor grew up, he needed to rely on his eunuch to help him take back the power, but the power fell into the hand of the eunuchs. Most royal relatives and eunuchs were corrupted. They hurt good officials and people, and East Han went downhill gradually. During Han Ling Di's (汉灵帝) time, people were able to buy an official position with a fixed price.

Yellow Headband Army (黄巾军) During Ling Di's time, Xu Sheng (许生) from Kuaiji (会稽) led an uprising at Juzhang (句章) (now Cixi, Zhejiang). There were over 10 thousand people followed him. They defeated army and became a big force. But in 174 AD, they were perished. There were three brothers from Julu County (巨鹿郡) (now Pingxiang, Hebei), Zhang Jiao (张角), Zhang Bao (张宝), and Zhang Liang (张梁). They decided to use religion as tool for uprising. They founded a religion, Taipingdao (太平道). Zhang Jiao knew medicine and often he helped people to treat illness for free. They accepted some disciples and asked them to preach, heal sickness, and organize people. About 10 years, Taipingdao was all over the nation, had about few hundred thousand followers. Someone told Ling Di, but he didn't put it in mind. Taipingdao followers agreed to uprise on March 5 of Jiazinian (甲子年) [Chinese year] (184 AD), but more than one month before the agreed day, a traitor informed the official. Over one thousand people were killed at Luoyang. Zhang Jiao decided to advance the uprising day to February. Everyone joined the uprising should wear yellow head band to be recognized. They were the Yellow Headband Army (YHA). Ling Di asked his brother-in-law He Jin (何进) to calm the riot, but because the involved area was so large, he ordered every place to protect by itself. Nine months later, Zhang Jiao died from illness. Zhang Bao and Zhang Liang were died later. The main motive force of uprising was gone, YHA was disintegrated to small forces and continued its fight for 20 years.

In 189 AD, Ling Di died, his 14 years old son, Liu Bian (刘辩) became the emperor, Han Shao Di (汉少帝). His mother, Empress Dowager He, help him manage the nation. His uncle, Commander-in-chief He Jin, was in power. He Jin's subordinate, Yuan Shao (袁绍), suggested him to eliminate the eunuchs. Empress Dowager He disagreed, but He Jin decided to invite Bingzhoumu (并州牧) (head of Bingzhou in charge of (now) most Shanxi, inner Mongolia, and part of Hebei) Dong Zhuo (董卓) for help. This plot was known by the eunuchs. They killed He Jin. After Dong Zhuo entered Luoyang, the power fell into his hand. He abolished Shao Di, set his brother, Liu Xie (刘协), as the emperor, Han Xian Di (汉献帝). He himself became the prime minister.

Cao Cao (曹操) was a native of Peiguoqiaoxian (沛国谯县) (now Bo, Anhui). When he was 20 years old, he was in charge of the public safety at the northern part of Luoyang. He noticed that Dong Zhuo wasn't welcomed by people and would fall. He returned to Chenliu (陈留) (now Chenliu, Henan, 20 km southeast of Kaifeng). With his father's agreement, he started to spend money on recruiting people and buying horses; ready to fight against Dong Zhuo. In 189 AD, Cao Cao and other against Dong Zhuo people gathered at Suanzao (酸枣), near Chenliu. They chose Yuan Shao as their leader. When Dong Zhuo knew what they did, he decided to move Xian Di and more than million people to Changan. He set a fire to burn down Luoyang, but the coalition didn't do anything. Everyone wanted to keep his force intact. Pretty soon, they used up their food and the coalition was dissolved. Cao Cao went to Yangzhou (扬州) (now south of Anhui's Huai River and Jiangsu's Yangtze River) to recruit people.

At Changan, Dong Zhuo was more domineering. In 192 AD, Prime Minister Wang Yun (王允) collaborated with Dong Zhuo's stepson, Lu Bu (吕布) killed Dong Zhuo at the palace. The power of Cao Cao grew bigger and bigger. In 195 AD, Xian Di went back to Luoyang, but no one came to help him. Cao Cao was at Xucheng (许城) (now Xuchang, Henan). His subordinates suggested him to welcome Xian Di to Xucheng. In 196 AD, Cao Cao made the invitation and Xian Di agreed to move the capital to Xucheng and changed its name to Xudu (许都). Cao Cao named himself be the Commander-in-chief. He used Xian Di's name to give orders. Cao Cao asked soldiers to do the farming and solved the food supply problem.

Liu Bei (刘备) was a native of Zhuojun (涿郡) (now Beizhuo, Hebei). He was an offspring of West Han royal family. Once, he was the head of Xuzhou (徐州牧). He went to work for Cao Cao. Together, they defeated Lu Bu. Cao Cao respected Liu Bei very much. At the meantime, Xian Di felt the power of Cao Cao was too great. He secretly summoned his uncle (on his mother side) Dong Cheng (董承) to get rid of Cao Cao. Dong Cheng contacted Liu Bei for this issue. Right at this moment, Liu Bei received an order from Cao Cao, asking him to attack Xuzhuo. Upon receiving the order, Liu Bei left right away. He took Xuzhuo and rebelled against Cao Cao, not to return Xudu. Cao Cao sent troop to attack Liu Bei. Liu Bei went to follow Yuan Shao. In 200 AD, Yuan Shao dispatched 100 thousand soldiers to attack Cao Cao. He was defeated at Guandu (官渡). Cao Cao spent the next 7 years to clean up the rest forces of Yuan Shao. Liu Bei fled to Jingzhou (荆州) to be with Liu Biao (刘表). At Jingzhou, Liu Bei found Zhuge Liang (诸葛亮) and used him as his military advisor.

Dongwu (东吴) Sun Ce (孙策) was son of Sun Jian (孙坚), the head of Changsha (长沙太守). After Sun Jian died, Sun Ce went to follow Yuan Shu (袁术). One time, Sun Ce requested to go to Danyang (丹阳) (now Xuancheng, Anhui) to help his uncle (on his mother side). Yuan Shu gave him one thousand soldiers. On his way, many people followed him, and he had 5-6 thousand men. He not only took back Danyang, he also conquered 6 counties at Jiangdong (江东) area. Unfortunately, Sun Ce was killed by an enemy's arrow during a hunting trip. His 19 years old brother, Sun Quan (孙权), took over his position. With the help of Zhang Zhao (张昭), Zhou Yu (周瑜) and Lu Su (鲁肃), Sun Quan established Dongwu.

Battle of Chibi (赤壁之战) After Cao Cao calmed down the northern territory, in 208 AD, he led a large army to attack Jingzhou. At this time, Liu Biao was already passed away. His son, Liu Cong (刘琮), surrendered. Liu Bei was defeated by Cao Cao. Liu Bei and Sun Quan united to fight against Cao Cao. Liu Bei had 20 thousand navy and Sun Quan had 30 thousand navy, but Cao Cao had 200 thousand soldiers, claimed to be 800 thousand. Cao Cao had problems – his soldiers were not good at fighting in water and some Jingzhou soldiers were not loyal to him. At Chibi (赤壁), the soldiers of Liu Bei and Sun Quan used fire to burn up Cao Cao ships, which were connected together. Cao Cao was defeated and Jingzhou was recovered. This started a period of China ruling by three independent powers.

After battle at Chibi, Liu Bei went to conquer Yizhou (益州) (now Sichuan, Yunnan, and part of Shaanxi, Gansu, Hubei, Guizhou). He shared Jingzhou with Dongwu, using Xiangshui (湘水) as their boundary. Then, Liu Bei took Hanzhong (汉中). In 209 AD, he became Hanzhong Wang (汉中王). He sent Guan Yu (关羽) to attack the central plain area. When he almost reached Xudu, Cao Cao contacted Sun Quan to fight Guan Yu together. Sun Quan agreed. He sent Lu Meng (吕蒙) to sneak attack Jingzhou. At the meantime, Cao Cao started his counterattack. Guan Yu was defeated and killed.

Zhang Heng (张衡) (78-139 AD) Zhang Heng was a famous scholar in literature and science during East Han. During Han An Di's (汉安帝) time, he was responsible of Astronomy. He made a celestial globe (浑天仪), a model for the movement of sun, moom, and stars. He also made a seismograph (地动仪) can be used to detect where an earthquake happened.

Cai Lun (蔡伦) In 105 AD, Cai Lun improved the method of making paper. He used bark, hemp head, rag, and old fishing net as raw materials to make paper. It greatly reduced the cost of making paper. At the meantime, it increased the paper quality and quantity. Paper gradually replaced bamboo slips and silk cloth. [14]

I.11 Three kingdoms (三国): Wei, Shuhan, and Dongwu [2, 4]

I.11.1 Wei (魏朝) 220-265 AD: It had 5 kings, total 46 years. After Cao Cao died, Han Xian Di resigned and Cao Pi (曹丕), Cao Cao's son, became the king, Wei Wen Di (魏文帝). Grand General Sima Yi (司马懿) was sent to attack Shuhan, Guanzhong, and Liaodong (辽东). Power fell into his hand. After he died, his son took over. Later, his grandson, Sima Yan (司马炎) abolished Wei Yuan Di (魏元帝) and established Jin Dynasty.

I.11.2 Shuhan (蜀汉) 221-263 AD: It had 2 kings, total 43 years. After Cao Pi claimed to be the king, Liu Bei, in 221 AD, also claimed to be the king, Han Zhaoli Di (汉昭烈帝). After he became the king, he attacked Dongwu for the revenge of loss Jingzhou and Guan Yu, although most his men disagreed this action. In few months, he gained 500-600 li [about 210-250 km] territory of Dongwu. He made dozens of large camps, using wood fence to connect the camps. Half year later, Lu Xun (陆逊) used fire to attack his camps. He was defeated. Soon, he died of illness. His son, Liu Shan (刘禅) became the king, Houzhu (后主) [the last king]. Zhuge Liang helped him to manage the nation. Zhuge Liang arrested Meng Huo (孟获) 7 times and calmed down the internals. He made 4 attacks at Wei but failed. Later, he was sick and died. Soon, Shuhan was perished by Wei.

I.11.3 Dongwu (东吴) 222-280 AD: It had 4 kings, total 59 years. After Sima Yan became the king, Dongwu became weak. In 279 AD, Jin Dynasty sent over 200 thousand soldiers to attack Dongwu by 3 routes. Dongwu surrendered and perished.

I.12 Jin Dynasty (晋朝) [2, 4] Jin Dynasty can be divided into two periods: West Jin and East Jin.

I.12.1 West Jin 265-316 AD: It had 4 kings, total 52 years. Sima Yan, Jin Wu Di (晋武帝), led people to have luxury life. The whole nation sank into the dissolute lifestyle. Wu Di, his father, and his grandfather, were all master of trickery, but his son was a man with low capability. In order to have a stable monarch power, he assigned 27 his family relatives with the same last name to be the noble kings. After Wu Di died, his son Sima Zhong (司马衷) became the emperor, Jin Hui Di (晋惠帝). Noble kings fought each other, causing the chaos fighting between the 8 noble kings, lasted 16 years. The unrest at the central plain area, plus nature disasters, many people left their home and became refugee. In 298 AD, Guanzhong had famine, over 100 thousand refugees fled to Shu (蜀地) (now Sichuan). At this time, the minority at north were mainly Xiongnu (匈奴), Xianbei (鲜卑), Jie (羯), Di (氐), and Qiang (羌) five ethnic groups. They took the advantage of the the fighting among 8 noble kings, entered the central plain area and fought against Jin Dynasty. Among them, Liu Yuan (刘渊), a native of Xiongnu, in 304 AD, led 50 thousand people to the central plain area to help the army of Jin fighting the Xianbei. Soon, he became a king, Han Wang (汉王). In 308 AD, he claimed to be the emperor at Pingyang (平阳) (now Linfen, Shanxi). When he died, his son, Liu Cong (刘聪) became the king. He took Luoyang. Next year, he killed Jin Huai Di (晋怀帝). Jin Min Di (晋愍帝) took throne at Changan. In 316 AD, Liu Cong conquered Changan and killed Min Di. West Jin Dynast was perished.

When Liu Cong's son, Liu Yao (刘曜), became the king, he changed title of his kingdom to Zhao (赵) (Pre-Zhao). In 328 AD, Grand General Shi Le (石勒) killed Liu Yao and became the king. The title of his nation was still Zhao (赵) (Post-Zhao). Shi Le was a native of Jie. He didn't have any education, but he respected intellectuals and he was willing to learn.

After Luoyang fell, some generals of West Jin continued to fight at the north. In 308 AD, Hui Di named Liu Kun (刘琨) to be the head of Bingzhou (并州刺史). At that time, Bingzhou was taken by enemy, people escaped to other places. Liu Kun recruited over one thousand people. They conquered Jingyang (晋阳) (now Taiyuan southwest, Shanxi). Liu Kun led people to rebuild Jingyang. He was named Grand General by Min Di. He stayed at Jingyang until Changan fell. Zu Yi (祖逖) was a good friend of Liu Kun. After Luoyang fell, he bought some people fled to the south. He suggested Sima Rui (司马睿) to fight in the north. He believed people at north would support them, but Sima Rui didn't intend to recover the central plain area. He named Zu Ti the head of Yuzhou (豫州刺史) (now Henan southeast and Anhui north), gave him food supply for one thousand men, and 3 thousand rolls of cloth. The rest was Zu Ti's job to prepare. Zu Ti led a group people went north, across the Yangtze River. He sworn that he would not come back, if he couldn't take the central plain area. At

Huaiyang (淮阳) (now Zhoukou, Henan), he started making weapon and recruiting people.

Zu Ti, later, led two thousand men to fight north. On the way, he received many supports from the people. He persuaded people not to fight against each other, but the enemy. In 319 AD, he attacked Chenliu (20 km southeast of Kaifeng, Henan). Shi Le sent 50 thousand soldiers to counter the attack but was defeated. Zu Ti recovered an area south of Yellow River. Zu Ti was named Zhenxi General (镇西将军). Zu Ti encouraged farming and worked with his subordinates. When he was ready to continue fight north, he was stopped by Yuan Di (Sima Rui), who sent Dai Yuan (戴渊) to take ove his position. Later, Zu Ti died of anxiety and illness.

I.12.2 East Jin (东晋) 317-420 AD: It had 11 kings, total 104 years. Before Jin Min Di was captured, he ordered Sima Rui (司马睿) who stationed at Jiankang (建康) (now Nanjing, Jiangsu) to be the emperor. In 317 AD, Sima Rui became the emperor, Jin Yuan Di (晋元帝), started the East Jin Dynasty. After Zu Ti died, internal fighting continuously happened at East Jin；Wang Dun (王敦) attacked Jiankang and killed people against him; when Ming Di (明帝) became emperor, he attacked Jiankang again, but failed and died in illness; during Cheng Di's (成帝) time, Liyang (历阳) (now He, Anhui) General Su Jun (苏峻) rebelled. He attacked Jiankang. Tao Kan (陶侃), head of Jingzhou (荆州刺史), fought against him. After two years, the rebellion ceased.

Huan Wen's north expedition (桓温) After Tao Kan calmed down the rebellion of Su Jun, some internal fighting happened at Post-Zhao in the north. After Shi Hu (石虎), son of Shi Le, died, Xianbei's noble, Murong Jun (慕容俊), took over the nation and established Pre-Yan (前燕). Fu Jian (苻健), a native of Di, siezed the opportunity, took Guanzhong, and established Pre-Qin (前秦). General Huan Wen (桓温) wrote to Jin Mu Di (晋穆帝) suggested to fight the north. Mu Di didn't trust Huan Wen. He asked Yin Hao (殷浩) to lead the north expedition but failed. Huan Wen asked for north expedition the 2nd time. Mu Di granted his request. He led 40 thousand men, separated in 3 routes, went north. He defeated Fu Jian's 50 thousand troop and went all the way to Changan. But he retreated, because of inadequate food supply. He did two more north expeditions. During the last fighting, he attacked Pre-Yan, all the way to Fangtou (枋头) (now Jun west, Henan). He retreated, because the food supply line was cut off. Later, Huan Wen took over the power, abolished the emperor, Mu Di's cousin Sima Yi (司马奕), and set Sima Yu (司马昱) to be the emperor. He himself became the Prime Minister.

Battle of Feishui (淝水之战) After Fu Jian died, his son Fu Sheng (苻生) became the king. He was cruel and was overthrown by his cousin, Fu Jian (苻坚). Fu Jian was a capable man. He named himself Da Qin Tian Wang (大秦天王). He used Wang Meng (王猛), a 36 years old young man of Han, to be his Prime Minister and Commander of his troop. Over ten years, his Pre-Qin kingdom, became a strong nation, defeated Pre-Yan, Daiguo (代国), Pre-Liang (前凉), occupied the area around the Yellow River. In 375 AD, Wang Meng was seriously ill. Before he died, he advised Fu Jian not to attack Jin, but to wipe out Xianbei and Qiang first. Three years after Wang Meng died, Fu Jian dispatched over 100 thousand soldiers to attack Jin, with his son Fu Pi (苻丕), Murong Chui (慕容垂, a native of Xianbei), and Yao Chang (姚苌, a native of Qiang), etc. as leaders. After one year, they captured Xiangyang (襄阳) (now Xiangyang, Hubei) and its General Chu Xu (朱序). Fu Jian didn't kill Chu Xu and kept him as his subordinate. But he was defeated badly, when he tried to attack Huainan (淮南) (now Huainan, Anhui). In 382 AD, Fu Jian was ready to attack Jin again, although all his officials except Murong Chui disagreed the move. In August, he led 870 thousand soldiers from Changan to attack Jin. Xie An (谢安) was the Prime Minister of East Jin. He commanded his brother, Xie Shi (谢石), as Commander and his nephew, Xie Xuan (谢玄) as Forward, led 80 thousand Beifubing (北府兵) to counter the attack. After taking Shouyang (寿阳) (now in Anhui), Fu Jian asked Chu Xu to persuade Jin's army to surrender. Chu Xu on the contrary told Xie Shi the military situation of Qin's army and advised him to attack Qin's army as soon as possible, not to wait for more Qin's army to come. Therefore, Jin's army started to attack Qin's army and won at Luojian (洛涧). Two forces faced each other at Feishui (淝水). Xie Xuan sent a message to Fu Jian, asking him to backup little bit, so that there was room for two forces to fight. Fu Jian agreed. But when Fu Jian's army starting to backup, they could not be stopped. At tail end of Qin's army, Chu Xu shouted: "Qin is defeated!" This caused Qin's soldiers to run away from the battlefield. Jin's army marched forward to chase them and Qin was defeated badly. This was the Battle of Feishui.

Liu Yu (刘裕) was a poor little officer. Later, he controlled the power of East Jin. He was not a noble. In order to raise his prestige, he decided to fight the north. In 409 AD, he defeated Nan Yan (南燕). Few years later, he defeated Post-Qin (后秦). In 420 AD, Jin An Di (晋安帝) died. Liu Yu persuaded Jin Gong Di (晋恭帝) to resign and he himself became the emperor, Song Wu Di (宋武帝). It started the history of North and South Dynasty.

I.13 North and South Dynasty (南北朝) South Dynasty had four

dynasties: Song, Qi, Liang, and Chen. North Dynasty was North Wei. Later it splitted to East Wei and West Wei. Later, East Wei became North Qi and West Wei became North Zhou. [2. 4]

I.13.1 South Dynasty

Song (宋) 420-479 AD: It had 8 kings, total 60 years. When the 3rd king of South Song, Song Xiao Wu Di (宋孝武帝), took throne, its nation already corrupted and went downhill. In 479 AD, Xiao Wu Di died. Xiao Dao-cheng (萧道成), Head of Nanyanzhou (南兖州刺史), took over the nation and became the king, named the nation Qi(齐). He was Qi Gao Di (齐高帝).

Zu Chongzhi (祖冲之) Zu Chongzhi liked to study Math and Astronomy. Song Xiao Wu Di assigned him to do research. He invented a new calender (Daming calender), a compass cart, a boat could travel 50 km a day, using water force to grind grains, and Pi to the 7th position after the decimal. He was a great inventor.

Qi (齐) 479-502 AD: It had 7 kings, total 24 years. Many people believed in Buddhism. After Qi Gao Di and Wu Di, internal fighting broke out. In 501 AD, Xiao Yan (萧衍), head of Yongzhou (雍州刺史), took over Qi and established Liang Dynasty (梁), Liang Wu Di (梁武帝).

Liang (梁) 502-557 AD: It had 4 kings, total 57 years. Whe North Wei had internal fighting, several times, Liang Wu Di went to north to fight, but all failed. Liang Wu Di was very generous to royal family and nobles, but very strict to his people. This led to officials living in luxurious life and people in poor life. Liang Wu Di believed Buddhism. Four times, he planned to be a monk, but he was redeemed back by using large amount of money. Before his 4th try to be a monk, he had a dream. In the dream, an official from the north came to follow him. After over 20 days, West Wei's Grand General Hou Jing (候景) came to surrender and was also willing to give him 13 states. (Hou Jing was East Wei's Grand General.) Liang Wu Di thought it was a good chance to recover the central plain. He sent his nephew, Xiao Yuanming (萧渊明) led 50 thousand soldiers to respond to Hou Jing. But he was defeated by the army of East Wei and was captured. East Wei notified Liang Wu Di, willing to exchange Xiao Yuanming with Hou Jing. Liang Wu Di agreed. This plot was known by Hou Jing. He led his men across the Yangtze River and fought all the way to Jiankang. After over 130 days fighting, Jiankang fell and Liang Wu Di was captured. He was put under house arrest and was died of hungry. After Wu Di died, Hou Jing set up two puppy kings. In 551 AD, he became king himself. Hou Jing killed and robbed people and made a great disaster. Next year, South Liang's Grand General, Chen Ba Xian (陈霸先) led his troop, defeated Hou Jing. In 557 AD, he became the king at Jiankang, Chen Wu Di (陈武帝).

Chen (陈) 557-589 AD: It had 5 kings, total 33 years. At this time, the north was in chaos and South Chen was gradually stable and settled down. South Chen's 5th king, Chen Houzhu (陈后主) was very absurd. He totally didn't know nation's affairs, but how to enjoy life. In 588 AD, Sui Wen Di (隋文帝) sent his son Yang Guang (杨广) and Prime Minister Yang Su (杨素) as marshal, led 510 thousand soldiers through 8 routes to attacked South Chen, perished it and united China.

I.13.2 North Dynasty

North Wei (北魏) 386-534 AD: It had 11 kings, total 149 years. In 439 AD, North Wei Tai Wu Di (太武帝) united the north. Xiao Wen Di (孝文帝) worked on reform, moved capital to Luoyang, used Han's language, wore Han's clothes, and married to Han people. He even changed his surname from 'Tuoba' (拓跋) to 'Yuan' (元). Xiao Wen Di attacked South Qi twice but didn't win. After Xiao Wen Di, North Wei went downhill.

East Wei (东魏) 534-550 AD: It had 1 king, total 17 years. In 534 AD, North Wei had internal fighting. Gao Huan (高欢) at Luoyang set Xiao Jing Di (孝静帝) as the king. North Wei became East Wei.

West Wei (西魏) 535-557 AD: It had 3 kings, total 23 years. In 534 AD, Xiao Wu Di fled to Changan to rely on Yuwen Tai (宇文泰), established West Wei.

North Qi (北齐) 550-577 AD: It had 6 kings, total 28 years. When South Chen Wu Di became king, East Wei was taken over by Gao Yang (高洋), son of Gao Huan. Gao Yang established North Qi.

North Zhou (北周) 557-581 AD: It had 5 kings, total 25 years. In 557 AD, Yuwen Jue (宇文觉), son of Yuwen Tai, took over West Wei, established North Zhou, and became the king; Xiaomin Di (孝闵帝). North Zhou and North Qi fought against each other. Later, North Zhou Wu Di (武帝) defeated North Qi, unified the north. Wu Di was a wise and capable king. After he died, Xuan Di (宣帝) became the king. Xuan Di was a tyrant. After he died, the power fell into the hand of his father-in-law, Yang Jian (杨坚). In 581 AD, Yang Jian made himself to be the king, changed national title to Sui (隋), Sui Wen Di (隋文帝).

I.14 Sui Dynasty (隋) [2, 4] 581-618 AD: It had 4 kings, total 38 years.

In 589 AD, Sui Wen Di unified China. He reformed the system of officials and military, implemented imperial examination, punished corruption strictly, and abolished cruel punishment. He was very thrift. His son, Jin Wang (晋王) Yang Guang (杨广) was very cunning. He pretended to be very thrift and won his father's trust to make him as the crowned prince. After Wen Di died, Yang Guang became the emperor, Sui Yang Di (隋炀帝). He was a very luxurious emperor. After he became the emperor, he started two big building projects: building palace at Dongdu (now Luoyang, Henan) as the eastern capital and building a canal to connect the south and the north. He used several million people to work on these projects. Every year, he would travel for inspection and people had to pay his expenses. At one time, he traveled to the north. He used over a million people to repair the Great Wall and he set a deadline of 20 days for this work. In 611 AD, he sent more than a million men to attack Koryo (高丽) (now Korea), only 2700 people came back alive. One year later, he started another attack at Koryo. Yang Xuangang (杨玄感), son of Yang Su, led 8 thousand labors to rebel, used Li Mi (李密) as his advisor, attacking Dongdu. Many people joined him, and their number reached 100 thousand. But this rebel failed and Yang Xuangang was killed.

Wagang Army (瓦岗军) Zhai Rang (翟让) was Wagang Army's (瓦岗军) leader. He was a low rank official. Once, he offended his boss and was put in jail. A guard set him free. He led an uprising at Wagangzhai (瓦岗寨) (now Hua southeast, Henan). Soon, he had over 10 thousand people. Li Mi joined him, helped him organizing his troop. They first took Xingyang (荥阳). Then, they took the large granary close to Dongdu. They opened the barn and distributed food to people. Zhai Rang considered Li Mi was more capable than he, so he let Li Mi to take over his position. But Zhai Rang's men disagreed. Later, Li Mi killed Zhai Rang. From this point on, Wagang Army went downhill. But another uprising army led by Li Yuan (李渊) was rising at the north.

Li Yuan was a noble of Sui Dynasty. In 617 AD, he was in charge of Taiyuan (太原), suppressing the riots. One time, he fought against Tujue (突厥) and was defeated. His 2nd son, Li Shimin (李世民) advised him to rebel against Sui Dynasty. He agreed. He led his army advancing westward and took Changan. He set Yang Di's grandson, Yang You (杨侑), as the emperor. Later, Yang Di was retreated to Jiangdu (江都) (now Yangzhou, Jiangsu). In 618 AD, Guard Army rebelled and Yang Di was killed. Li Yuan abolished Yang You, took the thorne, and became the emperor, Tang Gao Zu (唐高祖), named the national title Tang (唐).

I.15 Tang Dynasty (唐朝) 618-907 AD: It had 20 kings, total 290 years. In 620 AD, Tang Gao Zu sent Li Shimin to attack Dongdu. Dou Jiande (窦建德) led 300 thousand Hebei uprising army to rescue Dongdu but was defeated. [2,4]

Xuanwumen incident (玄武门之变) Tang Gao Zu set his eldest son Li Jiancheng (李建成) to be the crowned prince, but because Li Shimin made great accomplishment, Jiancheng and his 3rd brother Li Yuanji (李元吉) united together planning to kill Shimin. Li Shimin complained their plot to Gao Zu. Gao Zu agreed to check this issue the next day. In the morning of the next day, Li Shimin killed both of his brothers at city gate Xuanwumen (玄武门) at the north side of the palace. This was the incident of Xuanwumen. Two months later, Gao Zu handed over his throne to Li Shimin, Tang Taizong (唐太宗).

Zhenguan Era (贞观之治) Tang Taizong was an open-minded king. He wouldn't keep grudge against people, liked to use talents, and able to accept officials' suggestion. He reduced people's labor work and encourage production. The nation became more stable. This was called the Era of Zhengguan. Zhengguan was the reign title used by Taizhong.

Sanzang retrieved Buddhism scriptures (三藏取经) Master Sanzang (三藏法师) Xuanzang (玄奘) was a monk at Dacien Temple (大慈恩寺) in Changan. In 627 AD, he left Changan to Tianzhu (天竺) (now India) to retrieve Buddhism scriptures. After many difficulties, in 645 AD, he brought over 600 Buddhism scriptures back to Changan.

Princess Wencheng (文成公主) During the time of Tang Taizhong, China was very strong. He defeated East Tujue (东突厥) and was called Tian Kehan (天可汗) by all the tribes at the northwest area. Later, he defeated Tuguhun (吐谷浑) (now Qinghai Province). It opened the route to western countries. Many of them came to visit Tang Dynasty. Tufan (吐蕃) were Tibetan's ancestor, living at Qinghai-Tibet Plateau. Its king Songtsan Gambo (松赞干布) was knowledgeable and also good at martial art. He sent diplomats to Changan to make friend with Tang Dynasty. Taizong also sent diplomats to visit Tibet. Two years later, Songtsan Gambo sent an envoy to Changan asking to establish monarh marriage relationship. Taizhong didn't agree. Gambo's envoy lied to Gambo, said that Tang agreed the marriage, but because of Tuguhun also asking for monarch marriage, so Tang delayed Tibet's request. Tufan and Tuguhun were not friendly to each other. After hearing envoy's explanation, Gambo sent 200 thousand men to attack Tuguhun and won. Then, he advanced his troop to Songzhou (松州) (now Songpan, Sichuan), Tang's territory. Taizhong sent troop to fight. Later, they agreed to reconcile. Four years later, Gambo sent Ludongzan (禄东赞), a capable envoy, to Changan to ask monarch marriage again. This time, Ludongzan brought over 100 men, 1000 liang (两) gold [500 kg] and many jewelries with him. Taizhong selected a beautiful and gentle princess from the royal family, Princess Wencheng (

文成公主) to marry to Songtsan Gambo. In 641 AD, 24 years old Princess Wencheng went to Tufan to marry Gambo, carried with her many dowry, including grain, seed, medicine, silkworm, and various books. Princess Wencheng stayed in Tibet for 40 years, made great contribution the friendly relationship between Han and Tibet. In 650 AD, Songtsan Gambo passed away. One year before, Taizhong also passed away. His son, Li Zhi (李治) became the emperor, Tang Gaozhong (唐高宗).

Wu Zetian (武则天) Gaozhong was an ordinary incompetent man. He relied on his uncle (on his mother side) and Prime Minister Gongsun Wuji (公孙无忌) to handle nation affairs. Wu Zetian was Taizhong's concubine. When Taizhong died, she was sent to a nunnery. Gaozhong noticed her when he was a prince. Two years later, Gaozhong took her back from the nunnery. Later, Gaozhong made her the Empress. After she became the Empress, she started to eliminate people against her. Soon, Gaozhong was sick, Wu Zetian started to handle the nation's affairs. In 683 AD, Gaozhong passed away. Wu Zetian set her two sons to be the emperor, Li Xian (李显) to be Zhongzong (中宗) and Li Dan (李旦) to be Ruizhong (睿宗). Later, she abolished Zhongzong, put Ruizhong to house arrest, and took the power by herself. In September, 690 AD, 'upon the request of people', she became the emperor, changing the national title to Zhou. She was the only female emperor in Chinese history. In order to know who was against her, she encouraged people to tell other's secret. It caused many false accusation and injustice cases. In 705 AD, Wu Zetian was seriously ill. Prime Minister, Zhang Jianzhi (张柬之) and other officials seized the power. They welcomed Zhongzong to come back as the emperor.

Tang Xuanzong (唐玄宗) [He is also known as Tang Minghuang (唐明皇) to avoid using the word 'Xuan', because the name of Emperor Kangxi of Qing Dynasty is Xuanye.] During Zhongzong's time, Empress Wei was in power. The nation was in chaos. After Zhongzong died, Ruizong's son, Li Longji (李隆基), killed Empress Wei and supported Ruizong to be the emperor. Soon, Ruizong handed over his throne to his son, Li Longji, Tang Xuanzong, who was over 20 years old. Xuanzong disciplined his officials. Tang Dynasty was prospered. Over 20 years, he used talented people to manage the nation, leading to a peaceful nation. But, later, he started to enjoy life and was corrupted. He demoted the capable Prime Minister, Zhang Jiuling (张九龄), and used ignorant and incompetent Li Linfu (李林甫). Li Lingfu was Prime Minister for 19 years, and Tang Dynasty went downhill.

Yang Guifei (杨贵妃) When Xuanzong was 61 years old, he fell in love with Yang Guifei. He arranged two of her brothers to be high officials, three of her sisters to be his concubine, and her cousin, Yang Gaozhong (

杨国忠), to lead the royal Guard Army. Xuanzong let Li Linfu handled all nation's affairs and everyday he played with Yang Guifei.

Li Bai (李白) (701-762 AD) Li Bai is the most famous poet in China. Over 900 of his poems were kept today for people to enjoy. He was born in Xiyu (西域, the west) at Suiye (碎叶) (now Tokmok, Kyrgyztan). Before 25 years old, he studied in Shu (蜀) (now Sichuan). He was very open, generous, and good at fencing. Later, he liked to travel. At 42 years old, he went to Changan and did office work for Xuanzong for 3 years. He saw the corruption in the government. He resigned and started to travel again. In 756 AD, the next year of the An-Shi Rebellion, he went to follow Yong Wang (永王) Li Lin (李璘). Soon, Li Lin rebelled and was killed. Li Bai was punished to be sent to Yelang (夜郎). But amnesty exempted his punishment. It is not clear how he died. [4, 15]

An-Shi Rebellion (安史之乱) In order to protect its border, Xuanzong set up 10 Jiedushi (节度使) [military commander] at its border. According to the rule, Jiedushi was qualified to be Prime Minister. Li Linfu suggested using foreigner as Jiedushi, since they were brave. In fact, the reason was they were not qualified for Prime Minister. An Lushan (安禄山) was a low rank officer in the army of Pinglu (平卢) (now Chaoyang, Liaoning). He was sent to Changan, because he disobeyed military order and was defeated by enemy. Zhang Jiuling sentenced him to die, but Xuanzong pardoned him. After Zhang Jiuling left his office, An Lushan relied on flattery and became the Jiedushi of Pinglu, plus the Jiedushi at Fanyang (范阳) (now Beijing) and Hedong (河东) (now Taiyuan, Shanxi). After he gained trust of Xuanzong, he secretly expanded his troop, ready to rebel. After Li Linfu died, Yang Gaozhong became the Prime Minister. He and An Lushan had confrontation. In 755 AD, An Lushan sent 150 thousand soldiers from Fanyang going south. He met no resistance all the way to Luoyang. The first person raised up to fight against him was the head of Changshan (常山太守) (now Zhengding, Hebei), Yan Gaoqing (颜杲卿). He was a subordinate of An Lushan. He fought over ten day and failed. But it provided time for Tang Dynasty to move the troops. His bravery encouraged the moral to defeat the rebellion. One month after Yan Gaoqing was killed, Li Guangbi (李光弼) and Guo Ziyi (郭子仪) led their forces defeated the rebellion, recovered over 10 counties in Hebei. An Lushan was ready to return to Fanyang.

Tongguan (潼关) was the throat on the way to Changan. It was easy to keep and hard to attack. Geshuhan (哥舒翰) was there. Rebellion attacked it for half year but failed to take it. Yang Gaozhong was afraid that Geshuhan would defend Tongguan successfully, become a hero, and threatened his position as a Prime Minister. Therefore, he persuaded Xuanzong to order Geshuhan to attack the rebellion. Xuanzong didn't understand the consequence. He agreed Yang Gaozhong's suggestion. This helped the rebellion to attack and enter Tongguan. Then, quickly, the rebellion advanced to Changan. Xuanzong fled to Shu in a hurry. The 3rd day, they arrived Maweiyi (马嵬驿) (now Xingping west, Shaanxi). Soldiers killed Yan Gaozhong and requested to kill Yang Guifei. Xuanzong had no choice but agreed. Then, they fled to Chengdu (成都).

Prince Li Heng (李亨) left Maweiyi and went north. At Lingwu (灵武) (now Lingwu southwest, Ningxia), he took the throne as the emperor, Tang Suzong (唐肃宗). After heard Changan fell, Li Guangbi and Guo Ziyi returned to Taiyuan and Lingwu respectively. The recovered counties in Hebei fell into the hand of rebellion again.

Suzong invited his good friend, Li Mi (李泌) as his military advisor. Li Mi suggested Suzong to attack Hebei – the home of the rebellion. In the spring of the next year, An Qingxu (安庆绪), An Lusan's son, killed An Lusan. Suzong decided to attack Changan first. He sent Guo Ziyi to do the job. Guo Ziyi attacked Changan twice and took it. Later, Luoyang was also recovered. An Qingxu fled back to Hebei. Suzong sent 9 Jiedushi, led 600 thousand men to attack An Qingxu. Suzong was a suspicious man. He was afraid the army leader had too much power, so he sent a eunuch, Yu Zhaoen (鱼朝恩), who didn't know anything about military to control all the generals. This time, Tang army was defeated. Yu Zhaoen blamed Gao Ziyi for the defeat, released his duty, and replaced him by Li Guangbi. At this time, internal fighting happened at rebellion camp. Shi Siming (史思明) killed An Qingxu. He claimed to be the Big Yan Emperor (大燕皇帝) and went to attack Luoyang. Li Guangbi moved the people at Luoyang to Heyang (河阳) (now Meng, Henan). He defeated Shi Siming. Shi Siming fled back to Luoyang. Both sides facing each other for two years. Suzong used Yu Zhaoen's suggestion, ordered Li Guangbi to attack Luoyang. Tang army was defeated, and Li Guangbi was released from duty. Shi Siming was ready to attack Changan, but he was killed by his son, Shi Chaoyi (史朝义). The rebellion camp was splitted. Two years later, in 763 AD, Shi Chaoyi was defeated. This concluded the 8 years of An-Shi rebellion.

Zhang Xun (张巡) During An-Shi rebellion, the person protected Tang Dynasty, at the beginning, there was Yan Gaoqing, and later, there was Zhang Xun. Before the rebel advanced into Tongguan, An Lushan asked Linghu Chao (令狐潮) led 40 thousand men to attack Yunqiu (雍丘) (now Qi, Henan). The head of Zhenyuan (真源县), at Yunqiu nearby, recruited over one thousand men, occupied Yunqiu. He stayed at Yunqiu for over 60 days, resisted over 300 times rebel's attack, killed over half of the rebels, forced Linghu Chao to retreat. After Changan fell, Linghu Chao started another attack at Yunqiu, but Zhang Xun continued stay there and defeat the rebel. After one year, the head of Suiyang (睢阳) (now Shangqio, Henan), Xu Yuan (许远), made an emergency plea to Zhang Xun, because rebel's general, Yin Ziqi (尹子奇), led 130 thousand men to attack Suiyang. Zhang Xun came to help the fighting at Suiyang. Xu Yuan only had 6 thousand men, but they won the battle by defeated several attacks, killed enemy over 20 thousand. But Yin Ziqi came to attack Suiyang again. Only over one thousand six hundred men left at Suiyang, and they didn't have any food left. Zhang Xun sent Nan Jiyun (南霁云) led 30 cavalrymen to Linhuai (临淮) to ask for help, but the head of Linhuai (临淮太守) wasn't willing to help. At this time, onely four hundred men left at Suiyang. Zhang Xun still kept fighting at Suiyang, until the enemy broke into it and killed all the men there. Because of Zhang Xun kept fighting at Suiyang, area south of it didn't suffer any damage. This is a special patriotic tragedy history of Zhang Xun.

Guo Ziyi (郭子仪) After Suzong died, his son Li Yu (李豫) became the emperor, Daizong (代宗). Tufan united Tuguhun and other tribes with over 200 thousand men invaded China. They advanced into Changan. Daizong fled to Shaanzhou (陕州) (now Shaanxian, Henan), Daizong sent retired general Guo Ziyi to fight the enemy. Guo Ziyi didn't have soldiers, but his prestige scared the united Tufan army. Few years later, Tufan and Huihe (回纥) army of 100 thousand invaded China. When they closed to Jingyang (泾阳) (now Jingyang, Shaanxi) at the north of Changan. They met Guo Ziyi. Guo Ziyi noticed that these two enemies were not getting along well. He persuaded the general of Huihe, who was his subordinate before, to be his ally. When Tufan heard the news, they fled that night.

Border general and eunuch (藩镇与宦官) After An-Shi Rebellion, the power of Jiedushi (border general (藩镇)) increased. It formed many local powers. When Daizong died, his son Li Shi (李适), became the emperor, Dezong (德宗). In 782 AD, there were 5 border generals rebelled against government. Some generals defeated the largest border general, but Dezong was a suspicious person, he trusted and favored eunuch. It helped increasing the power of eunuch and it didn't solve the issue of areas to be controlled by border generals. In 805 AD, Dezong died, his son Li Song (李诵), who had stroke, became the emperor, Shunzong (顺宗). He used Wang Suwen (王叔文) rectified the order of his court, also corrected the corruption of the eunuch. Unfortunately, less than one year, the eunuch regained power. They set Prince Li Chun (李纯) as the emperor,

Xianzong (宪宗), stopped all the reform. Xianzong used some righteous people to manage the nation, but he still trusted in the eunuch. He continued fighting with border generals, but no success, after tried 3 years. In 817 AD, Li Su (李愬) was the Jiedushi of Tangzhou (唐州) (now Tanghe, Henan) and 2 other states. He defeated the border general at Huaixi (淮西). When Xianzong died, his son Li Heng (李恒) became the emperor, Muzong (穆宗). After Muzong, emperor was set by the eunuch and eunuch became very powerful.

Dispute between officials (朋党之争) When the eunuch was in power, the officials followed the eunuch were divided into two groups (with or without noble origin). They fought for 40 years. It ended until in 846 AD, when Xuanzong (宣宗) Li Chen (李忱) became the emperor.

Huang Chao (黄巢) Xuanzong was a clever emperor. The emperor after him, like Yizong (懿宗) and Xizong (僖宗) were very corrupt. People had hard time in living. Many chose to revolt. During Yizong's time, east of Zheijiang, there were 30 thousand people rose in rebellion. Eight years later, soldiers at Guilin uprising, reached 200 thousand men. These two uprisings were defeated later. Soon after Xizong became the emperor, there was a salt vendor, Wang Xianzhi (王仙芝) led few thousand peasants to rebel at Changyuan (长垣) (now Henan). Soon, Huang Chao (was an intellectual) led uprising at Shandong. These two rebels were later combined to one, led by Huang Chao. He first fought to the south, all the way to Guangzhou (广州). Then, he fought to the north. In 880 AD, he led 600 thousand men conquered Changan. He himself claimed to be the emperor, with national title Da Qi (大齐). His subordinate, Zhu Wen (朱温) surrendered to Tang Dynasty. Zhu Wen, Shatuo people(沙陀人), and, Jiedushi at Yanmengguan (雁门关), Li Keyong (李克用), led 40 thousand cavalrymen defeated 150 thousand uprising men at Changan. In 884 AD, Huang Chao died in the battle.

After Xizong died, his son Zhaozong (昭宗) became the emperor. He wanted to eliminate the eunuch. Zhu Wen helped him, but the power fell into the hand of Zhu Wen. Zhu Wen killed Zhaozong and set Zhaoxuan Di (昭宣帝) to be the emperor. In 907 AD, Zhu Wen killed Zhaoxuan Di and became the emperor himself. He changed the national title to Liang, and he was Hou Liang Taizu (后梁太祖). It started the period of Five Dynasties and Ten Kingdoms.

I.16 Five Dynasties and Ten Kingdoms (五代十国) [2, 4] Within the 50 years after Zhu Wen established Liang Dynasty, at the central plain, there were dynasties set up one after the other. They were Hou Liang (后梁),

Hou Tang (后唐), Hou Jin (后晋), Hou Han (后汉), and Hou Zhou (后周). They were the Five Dynasties. ['Hou' is added to the title of these dynasties to distinguish them from the ones established before.] At the south and Bashu (巴蜀) (now Sichuan), there were 9 kingdoms (Qianshu (前蜀), Wu (吳), Min (闽), Wuyue (吳越), Chu (楚), Nanhan (南汉), Nanping (南平), Houshu (后蜀), and Nantang (南唐)). Some of them claimed to an independent nation and some claimed to be a subordinate nation to the north. These nine kingdoms pluses the one in the north, Beihan (北汉), were the Ten Kingdoms. [2, 4]

I.16.1 Hou Liang (后梁) 907-923 AD: It had 2 kings, total 16 years.

When Zhu Wen established Liang Dynasty, there were two big forces at the central plain: Liu Rengong (刘仁恭) at Youzhou (幽州) and Li Keyong at Hedong (河东). After Li Keyong died, his son, Li Cunxu (李存勖) succeeded his position. He defeated Liu Rengong. In 923 AD, he defeated Liang Dynasty and united the north. He changed the national title to Tang. He was the Hou Tang Zhuangzong (后唐庄宗).

I.16.2 Hou Tang (后唐) 923-936 AD: It had 4 kings, total 14 years.

After Tang Zhuangzong took over the central plain, he put his heart in acting and started to use actors for important jobs. Few years later, his stepbrother, Li Siyuan (李嗣源), took over the throne, Tang Mingzong (唐明宗). After Mingzong died, his son Mo Di (末帝) become the emperor. He sent several 10 thousand army to attack his opponent, Hedong Jiedushi (河东节度使) Shi Jingtang (石敬瑭). Shi Jingtang begged help from Qidan's (契丹) Yelu Deguang (耶律德光). He also agreed to give great gifts for the help, which were to call Yelu Deguang his father (although Yelu Deguang was 10 years younger than he) and to give away the land of 16 states at Yanyun (燕云十六州) (now Hebei and Shanxi north). Mo Di committed suicide after heard the news. Shi Jingtang became the emperor. He changed the national title to Jin (晋). He was Hou Jin Gaozu (后晋高祖).

I.16.3 Hou Jin (后晋) 936-946 AD: It had 2 kings, total 11 years.

Shi Jingtang died, after being a shameful king of 7 years. His son Chu Di (出帝) became the emperor. He didn't get along well with Qidan. He was defeated by Qidan, and his kingdom perished. In 947 AD, Qidan entered the capital Bianjing (汴京), changed national title to Liao (辽). Liao's soldiers killed and robbed people. Many places fought against them. Yelu Denguang fled to his home. Jin's Grand General, Liu Zhiyuan (刘知远), took the throne and became the emperor, He changed the national title to Han (汉). He was Hou Han Gaozu (后汉高祖).

I.16.4 Hou Han (后汉) 947-950 AD: It had 2 kings, total 4 years.

Hou Han Gaozu was strict in discipline and people supported him. One year later, he died. Another 4 years later, Grand General Guo Wei (郭威) took the throne, became the emperor, changing the national title to Zhou. He was Hou Zhou Taizu (后周太祖).

I.16.5 Hou Zhou (后周) 951-960 AD: It had 3 kings, total 10 years. Hou Zhou Taizu was poor and understood the hardship of people. After he became the emperor, he disciplined his officials and turned around the situation at the central plain. He didn't have son. He considered the nephew of Empress Chai (柴皇后), Chai Rong (柴荣) as his son. After he died, Chai Rong became the emperor, Hou Zhou Shizong (后周世宗). At this time, Liu Zhiyuan's brother, Liu Chong (刘崇) took the throne as the king at Jinyang (晋阳), established the kingdom, Beihan (北汉). After Hou Zhou Taizou died, Liu Chong led 30 thousand men plus 10 thousand Liao's soldiers invaded the central plain. Hou Zhou Shizong led army to counter the attack. At Gaoping (高平) (now Shanxi), he defeated Liu Chong. Shizong disciplined his army, reducing tax, ready to unite the whole China. Two years later, he attacked Nantang, recovered 14 states at north of Yangtze River. Then, he fought in the north, recovered many places. But he sicked. In 960 AD, he died after 6 years at the throne. His son Gong Di (恭帝) was only 7 years old. At this time, Beihan and Liao came to invade again. Grand General Zhao Kuangyin (赵匡胤) led the army to fight. At Chenqiaoyi (陈桥驿), he was set as the emperor by his subordinates. He established Song Dynasty (宋朝). He was Song Taizu (宋太祖).

I.17 Song Dynasty (宋朝) Song Dynasty is divided into two periods: North Song and South Song. [2, 4]

I.17.1 North Song (北宋) 960-1127 AD: It had 9 kings, total 167 years.

Used one cup of wine to release military power (杯酒释兵权) Song Taizu thought the reason of the chaos of the Five Dynasties Period was the generals had too big power. It would be better, if these powers could be taken back and practicing power centralized in government. Therefore, one day, he invited all the old generals and told them his thinking. All the generals agreed to return their power to him and retired.

After regained military power, Taizu started to work on uniting China. He spent 13 years to perish the five nations at the south. Then, he attacked Beihan. Soon, he died. His brother took the throne. He was Song Taizong (宋太宗). Taizong perished Beihan. He also recovered some land from Liao. In 982 AD, Liao Jingzong (辽景宗) died, and Liao Shengzong (辽圣宗), only 12 years old, took the throne. Taizong decided to attack Liao to recover the 16 states of Yanyun, but he didn't success. At this time, there was uprising at Chuanshu (川蜀) area. It forced Taizong to concentrate to calm down the uprising.

Chanyuan Agreement (澶渊之盟) Soon after Taizong's son, Zhenzong (真宗), took the throne, Liao Shengzong led 200 thousand soldiers to attack Song. Prime Minister Kou Zhun (寇準) persuaded Zhenzong led troop to fight. Two armies facing each other at Chanzhou (澶州) (now Qingfeng, Henan). Kou Zhun wanted to fight, but Zhenzong preferred to reach a peaceful solution. In December 1004 AD, two sides reached an agreement, Song Dynasty would give Liao 200 thousand rolls of silk cloth, 100 thousand liang (兩) silver [50 thousand kg]. This was the Chanyuan Agreement.

After Chanyuan Agreement, Dangxiang tribe (党项族) at west border invaded Song. They occupied Ganzhou (甘州) and Liangzhou (凉州). Zhenzong also reached a peaceful solution with them by given them lots silk cloth and silver. After Zhenzong died, his son Renzong (仁宗) took the throne. After 10 years, the leader of Dangxiang tribe, Yuan Hao (元昊) defeated Tufan and Huihe, expanded his territory, and claimed to be the king of Da Xia (大夏). In 1038 AD, Yuan Hao attacked Song. Song had 300 to 400 thousand men guarding the west border, but they were scattered in 24 states. Therefore, Song's army was defeated repeatedly. Renzong sent Fan Zhongyan (范仲淹) and Han Qi (韩琦) to direct the troop at the west border. It improved the fighting. In 1043 AD, Yuan Hao agreed to be a subordinate under Song. Song also agree to give Da Xia some silk cloth and silver. This calmed down the western border.

Fan Zhonyan was a military specialist. He was also a politician and literature writer. He made 10 reform suggestions to Renzong. But when they were implemented, it met objection from the royal family and officials. The objection was so great, Fan Zhonyan resigned. Renzong stopped the reform. In the court, only Ouyang Xiu (欧阳修) defended Fan Zhonyan, but was demoted. Ouyang Xiu promoted reforming the literature style and was a famous literature writer. He, and Zeng Gong (曾巩), Wang Anshi (王安石), Su Xun (苏洵), Su Shi (苏轼), Su Zhe (苏辙), and Tang Dynasty's Han Yu (韩愈), Liu Zongyuan (柳宗元) were called the 8 masters of Song and Tang.

Renzong didn't have son. Yingzong (英宗) became the emperor. After 3 years, he died. His 20 years old son Shengzong (神宗) took the throne. Shengzong planned to reform. He used Wang Anshi's reform policy. It consolidated Song Dynasty, but it faced objection from the landlord and officials. Seven years after the reform, Wang Anshi resigned. Shengzong continued to use most of his reform policy for 13 more years until he died.

Shen Kuo (沈括) He was proficient in geography. During Shengzong's time, he went to Liao for negotiation to protect Song's territory intact. Once he used wax to make a three-dimensional map model. Shengzong asked him to make a map of the whole nation. He spent 14 years and finished the map. When he was old, he wrote a book, "Meng Xi Bi Tan" (梦溪笔谈) described his and others' invention. Among them, he mentioned Bi Sheng (毕升) invented clay type printing to replace the engraving (around 1045 AD, 400 years before the European invention).

Sima Guang (司马光) After Shengzong died, his 10 years old son Zhe-zong (哲宗) became the emperor. His grandmother, Empress Dowager Gao, was in power. She was against reform. Therefore, she used conservative Sima Guang as Prime Minister. Sima Guang specialized in studying history. During Yingzong's time, he started to write the history from the Warring States Period (403 BC) to the Five Dynasties (959 AD). He spent 19 years to finish his book, "Zi Zhi Tong Jian" (资治通鉴), a great writing.

Empress Dowager Gao died after 7 years in power. Zhezong managed the nation by himself. He emphasized in reform, but not as successful as before. His brother, Huizong (徽宗) took the throne after him. Huizong liked to have fun, not nation's affair. He collected many flower stones from the south. It caused the uprising at Qingxi (青溪) (now Chunan, Zhejiang). In less than 10 days, uprising army reached over several 10 thousand men, conquered over dozens of counties. Huizong sent eunuch Tong Guan (童贯) led 150 thousand men calmed down this revolt. Soon, there was uprising from Hebei, led by Song Jiang (宋江) and others 36 people. They fought from place to place at Qingzhou (青州), Qizhou (齐州), and Puzhou (濮州) areas (now Shandong).

Aguda (阿骨打) was the leader of Nuzhen tribe (女真族) at the northeast area. He didn't like the ruling of Liao and was ready to rebel. In 1115 AD, he claimed to be the king at Huining (会宁) (now Acheng south, Heilong-jiang). His national title was Da Jin (大金). He was Jin Taizu (金太祖). After he became the king, he attacked Huanglongfu (黄龙府) (now Nongan, Jilin) of Liao. Liao Tianzuo Di (辽天祚帝) sent 200 thousand ment to defend the attack but was defeated badly. Tianzuo Di requested for peace but was declined. Tianzuo Di sent another 700 thousand men to fight, but still was defeated badly. At this time, Jin Taizu talked to Song to fight Liao together. Song was responsible to attack Yanjing (燕京). If Song won the battle, it could recover the 16 states at Yanyuan, but Jin would receive the silk cloth and silver Song gave to Liao. After Tong Guan calmed the rebel at the south, he led 150 thousand men to attack Yanjing, but he was defeated twice. He asked help from Jin. Jin took Yanjing right away but refused to give it back to Song. Later, Tong Guang agreed to give the annual tax income of one millon liang silver [500 thousand kg] to Jin to buy back Yanjing.

The perish of North Song The fighting of Tong Guang at Yanjing, let Jin understand the fighting strength of Song. After Jin Taizu's brother, Jin Taizong (金太宗) became the king, he perished Liao. Then, he attacked Song through two routes. The west route, led by Zong Han (宗翰), attacked Taiyuan. The east route, led by Zongwang (宗望), attacked Yanjing. Then, these two routes would join at Bianjing. Huizong conceded his throne to Prince Qinzong (钦宗) and fled to Haozhou (亳州) (now Hao, Anhui). Song was defeated. Prime Minister Li Bangyan (李邦彦) persuaded Qinzong to fled and let the Minister of Military Affairs (兵部侍郎), Li Gang (李纲) to guard the capital. With the help of the Royal Guards, Li Gang prepared to protect Bianjing. He defeated Jin's attack and kept Bianjing safe. At meantime, Zhongshidao (种师道) led 200 thousand men to rescue Bianjing. The east route Jin only had 60 thousand men. They decided to retreat. Zhongshidao and Li Gang tried to sneak attack them but failed. Li Bangyan used this excuse to remove them from their positions. When this news reached the capital, several hundred students from the national institutes went to protest at palace. Soon, several 10 thousand people joined the protest. Qinzong had no choice, but to restore both men's position. Zhongshidao suggested to attack the retreated Jin soldiers but was rejected by Qinzong. Qinzong also removed him from his duty. After Jin retreated, Qinzong took Huizong back to the capital. At this time, the west route of Jin started attack Taiyuan. Li Gang went to rescue but failed. He was demoted to the south. Soon, Taiyuan fell. Two routes of Jin came to attack Bianjing. Qinzong sent his brother Kang Wang (康王) Zhao Gou (赵构) to negotiate for peace, but it was too late. Qinzong surrendered to Jin. Qingzong, Huizong, and 2-3 thousand royal family and officials were sent to the north as captives. This was the end of the North Song Dynasty. In 1127 AD, Kang Wang Zhao Gou became the emperor at Jiankang (建康) (now Nanjing). He was Song Gaozong (宋高宗), started the South Song Dynasty.

1.17.2 South Song (南宋) 1127-1279 AD: It had 9 kings, total 153 years.

Zong Ze (宗泽) He was a brave general fighting against Jin. Before the North Song perished, he tried hard to attack Jin's troop. When Gaozong took the throne, using Li Gang as his Prime Minister, Zong Ze was the head of Kaifeng Prefecture (开封知府). When he arrived Kaifeng, he set strict discipline to the troop. All the troops fighting Jin obeyed him. He defeated Jin Taizong's Grand General Wu Zhu (兀朮). He invited Gaozong to return Kaifeng to recover the central plain, but the message was intercepted by Gaozong's close aides. Zong Ze died when he was over 70 years old. The whole central plain fell to Jin again.

Han Shizhong (韩世忠) When Zong Ze went to Kaifeng, Gaozong and his close aides felt Jiankang was not safe and planned fled southward. Li Gang was against this idea and he was removed from office. Gaozong moved to Yangzhou (扬州). After Zong Ze died, spring of the next year, Jin attacked Yangzhou. Gaozong fled to Linan (临安) (now Hangzhou, Zhejiang). In the summer, Wu Zhu led 100 thousand Jin soldiers attack Song again. Gaozong fled to Wenzhou (温州). Wu Zhu was deep alone in Song's territory. So he looted the place and ready to return. At Zenjiang (镇江), he met Song's general, Han Shizhong. Han had only 8 thousand soldiers, but he badly defeated Wu Zhu. Wu Zhu fled back to Jiankang. Then, he was drove back to north by Yue Fei (岳飞).

Yue Fei (岳飞) Yue Fei was a famous general of South Song. He was Zong Ze's subordinate. He advocated to attack Jin to recover the central plain. He protected the nation and won many battles. He became a Jiedushi, when he was 32 years old. South Song had a group of brave generals, plus many local volunteer armies, it was possible for it to regain the central plain, but Gaozong chose to humiliate himself by begging Jin for peace. In 1193 AD, Gaozong agreed to be subordinate to Jin, giving Jin every year 250 thousand liang tribute silver [125 thousand kg], 250 thousand rolls silk cloth. Jin "returned" the land at Shaanxi and Henan area. Less than one year, Jin attacked southward, with Wu Zhu as the commander and using 4 routes. Gaozong had no choice. He commanded Yue Fei to fight against Jin. Yue Fei stayed at Yancheng (郾城) (now central Henan). Yue Fei contacted the volunteer army in Hebei to attack the enemy. Yue Fei defeated Jin badly at Yancheng. After few days, Wu Zhu led 120 thousand men to attack again, was also defeated. Yue Fei continued fighting northward, all the way to Zhuxiangzhen (朱仙镇), 45 li [19 km] from Bianjing. Many local volunteer armies responded to fight. The situation was favorable to South Song.

Qin Hui the traitor (秦桧卖国) Qin Hui was the captivated North Song high official during the fell of Bianjing. Later, Jin found that there were some capable generals in South Song. They decided to send Qin Hui to South Song as spy. Qin Hui made a fake story of how he run away from Jin. The Prime Minister of South Song, Fan Zongyin (范宗尹), was a friend of Qin Hui. In front of Gaozong, he said good words for Qin Hui. At the meantime, Gaozong was looking for someone to negotiate peace with

Jin. Gaozong decided to use Qin Hui. Less than one year, Qin Hui was in power. He wanted to have peace with Jin, and many officials were against him. But the ignorant Gaozong still trusted Qin Hui. When Yue Fei almost reached Bianjing during fighting, Qin Hui persuaded Gaozong to order Yue Fei to retreat. Gaozong continuously issued 12 golden cards ordered Yue Fei to retreat. Yue Fei had no choice but retreated. Once Yue Fei was retreated, Jin returned. Qin Hui took away Yue Fei's military power. Then, he negotiated with Jin. In November 1141 AD, Gaozong agreed to give Jin more land and continued the tributes. This was the Shaoxing (绍兴) Agreement. Jin was afraid of Yue Fei. They instructed Qin Hui to murder Yue Fei. Qin Hui made false accusation of Yue Fei, put Yue Fei in jail, and killed him. After Yue Fei died, someone stole his body and secretly buried him. After Gaozong died, the injustice to Yue Fei was corrected. People buried him at West Lake, built a temple to memory him.

Yu Yunwen (虞允文) After the Shaoxing Agreement, Song and Jin didn't fight for two years. Gaozong lived safely at south, totally forgot about the work of recovering central plain. During this period, something happened in Jin Dynasty. Wanyan Liang (完颜亮) killed Jin Xizong (金熙宗) and became the king himself. He was a tyrant and decided to attack South Song. This news leaked to Gaozong, but he didn't put it on his mind. In September 1161 AD, Wanyan Liang led 600 thousand soldiers to attack South Song, claiming to conquer South Song in 100 days. South Song's Chief General north of Yangtze River, Liu Qi (刘锜) was sick. His Deputy Commander, Wang Quan (王权), retreated to Caishi (采石) (now Maanshan southwest, Anhui). Prime Minister sent an official, Yu Yunwen, to greet the soldiers there. When Yu Yunwen went there, Wang Quan already left. The substitute general, Li Xianzhong (李显忠) had not arrived yet. Yu Yunwen was an intellectual, never involved in fighting, but facing the invading Jin army, he arranged how to fight. It was a big fight and Jin was defeated badly. At this time, the chief general Li Xianzhong arrived. They continued fighting against the Jin army. Jin soldiers started to fleed. Wanyan Liang was harsh to his subordinates, hoping to reverse the situation, but he was killed by his subordinates. Jin's army retreated. They supported Wanyan Yong (完颜雍) as the king, Jin Shizong (金世宗).

Xin Qiji (辛弃疾) When Wanyan Liang attacked South Song, many people in the north started to revolt. At Jinan (济南), Geng Jing (耿京) led a large uprising force of over 200 thousand men. Most of them were poor peasants. Xin Qiji was few of the intellectual among them. He became an important person to Geng Jing. Geng Jing sent him to accompany Jia Rui (贾瑞) to contact Gaozong at south. When they came back, Geng Jing was killed by traitors. Xin Qiji took the revenge for Geng Jing. Then, he went to the south to work, but he didn't get any important assignment. He wrote many ci (词) [one type of poem.] He was a patriotic ci writer.

Lu You (陆游) The year, when Xin Qiji came to see Gaozong, Gaozong resigned and his nephew, Zhao Shen (赵眘) became the emperor, Song Xiaozong (宋孝宗). Xiaozong intended to recover the central plain. He used Zhang Jun (张浚) to plan the north expedition. Zhang Jun asked Lu You to write a declaration for the north expedition. Lu You was a native of Shanyin (山阴) (now Shaoxing, Zhejiang), a famous patriotic poet. When Zhang Jun failed in the north expedition, Lu You resigned and returned home. After 10 years, Wang Yan (王炎), a general at Sichuan and Shaanxi, invited him to Hanzhong to be his staff to fight against Jin. He accepted the offer. The generals were not cooperating with each other, and there was no progress in fighting Jin. When Wang Yan was transferred to another place, Lu You was assigned to work in Chengdu (成都). At Chengdu, he started to write poem and using the pen name "Fangweng" (放翁). After 20-30 years, South Song had two emperors, Guangzong (光宗) and Ningzong (宁宗), but didn't recover its lost land. Lu You continued his writing. In 1206 AD, Prime Minister Han Tuozhou (韩侂胄) launched a large-scale north expedition but failed. Lu You was very sad.

Genghis Khan (成吉思汗) When Han Tuozhou failed in the north expedition, Jin Dynasty was going downhill. Mongolia became stronger. Mongolia was a subordinate nation to Jin Dynasty. In 1206 AD, tribes in Mongolia acknowledged Temujin (铁木真) as the Da Han (大汗) [king], claimed to be Genghis Khan. In the past, Jin killed Genghis Khan's ancestor. In 1211 AD, he took revenge and attacked Jin. Jin was badly defeated. Two years later, he attacked Juyongguan (居庸关) and entered Hebei. Jin asked for peace. In 1219 AD, Mongolian caravan went to the west. They were killed at Hualazimo (花拉子模) (now Caspian east, Aral Sea west). Genghis Khan led 200 thousand soldiers to fight, all the way to east Europe and north of Iran. Soon, Genghis Khan died. His son Ogadai (窝阔台) took the reign. In 1234 AD, Mongolia perished Jin Dynasty. Later, Mongolia and Song started to fight for the central plain. Afte Ogadai died, his nephew Mengge (蒙哥) took the reign. In 1258 AD, Mengge attacked South Song through three routes. Mengge attacked Hezhou (合州) (now Hechuan, Sichuan); his brother Kublai (忽必烈) attacked Ezhou (鄂州) (now Wuchang, Hunan); the 3rd route from Yunnan (云南) attack Tanzhou (潭州) (now Xiangtan, Hunan). When Mengge attacked Hezhou, he was killed. When Kublai attacked Ezhou, Lizong (理宗) sent Prime Minister Jia Sidao (贾似道) to rescue. Jia Sidao sent people to Kublai for peace. At first, Kublai didn't agree, but later he agreed, because he needed to go back to seize the throne. His conditions were north of Yantze River belonged to Mongolia and the annual tribute of silver and silk cloth should be at 200 thousand each. Jia Sidao didn't tell people about this peace agreement, but claimed he won the battle. Later, he refused to follow the peace agreement. Kublai went home and became the king, but his brother fought against him. Therefore, he had no time to deal with South Song.

Jia Sidao cheated the nation Jia Sidao cheated the nation, but he still served as the Prime Minister over ten years. When Lizong died, Duzong (度宗) became the emperor. After Kublai calmed down his internals, in 1271 AD, he claimed to be the emperor, with national title Yuan (元). He was Yuan Shizu (元世祖). He attacked Xiangyang (襄阳). Jia Sidao hid the fighting report of Xiangyang from Duzong. After Xiangyang fell, Mongolian soldiers went south. Jia Sidao could not hide his scam anymore. He asked peace but was refused. He run away.

Wen Tianxiang (文天祥) When Mongolian soldiers arrived Linan, Duzong already died, the new emperor was only 4 years old. Empress Dowager Xie (谢太后) and high officials sent out orders requested generals to rescue, but very few responded. Only the official of Ganzhou (赣州的州官) Wen Tianxiang and General Zhang Shijie (张世杰) at Yingzhou (郢州) (now Zhongxiang, Hubei) responded right away and came to help. When Wen Tianxiang was 20 years old, he won the 1st place in the national examination. He was patriotic but had not been assigned important position. At this time, the Prime Minister already fled. Wen Tianxiang was appointed as Prime Minister to Mongolian camp to negotiate peace. Wen Tianxiang refused to surrender, but Empress Dowager Xie agreed to surrender. In 1276 AD, Mongolian troop arrived Linan. South Song perished. Wen Tianxiang, Zhang Shijie, and Lu Xiufu (陆秀夫) continued fighting against Mongolia but failed. Wen Tianxiang was arrested, but he refused to surrender. In December 1282 AD, he was executed, only 47 years old.

I.18 Yuan Dynasty (元朝) 1279-1368 AD: It had 11 kings, total 90 years.

After Yuan Shizu united China, he developed more farmland and irrigation systems. The society was prospered, but only the ruling class was benefited, people still suffered. Yuan Dynasty classified its people into 4 classes: the 1st one was Mongolian, the 2nd one was Semu (color) (western area people) (色目人(西域人)), the 3rd was Han people (Jin people), and the 4th was Nan people (South Song people). These 4-class people had different political level and treatment. Han and Nan people were discriminated. After Shizu, Yuan Dynasty was corrupted. People started to uprising. In 1351 AD, Han Shantong (韩山童) and Liu Futong (刘福通) revolted at Yinshang (颍上) of Yinzhou (颍州) (now Fuyang, Anhui). They wore red turban and were called Red Turban Army. In less than 10 days, they had over 100 thousand men. Red Turban Army continued to expand. Two years later, they failed. [2, 4]

Zhu Yuanzhang (朱元璋) He wa a native peasant of Haozhou (濠州) (now Fengyang, Anhui). When he was 17 years old, his hometown had famine and plague. His family, except he and his 2nd brother, all died. He became a monk. Guo Zixing (郭子兴) organized a Red Turban Army at Haozhou. Zhu Yuanzhang joined him and was put in important position. Soon, he became the Commander, conquered Ying Tianfu (应天府) (now Nanjing). During 1360-1363 AD, he defeated his strong rivalry, Chen Youliang (陈友谅). Few years later, he united the south. In October 1367 AD, he attacked the north with 250 thousand soldiers. The same year, he claimed to be the emperor, with national title Ming. He was Ming Taizu (明太祖). In 1368 AD, Yuan Dynasty perished.

I.19 Ming Dynasty (明朝) 1368-1644 AD: It had 16 kings, total 277 years.

Taizu relied on his generals and advisors to unite China. There was one advisor, Liu Ji (刘基), also named Liu Bowen (刘伯温), advised Taizu should manage thing with grace and peace, but Taizu was cautious about his high officials. Later, he set up an office, Jinyiwei (锦衣卫) to check high officials' activities. It caused two big cases, killed about 50 thousand capable officials. It showed the cruelty of Taizu. [2, 4]

Ming Chengzu (明成祖) Taizu gave land to his sons and set them as the noble kings. They could keep troops. It was a plan to consolidate the ruling, but it caused a war. In 1398 AD, Taizu died. His grandson, Hui Di (惠帝) took the throne. He planned to reduce the military power of the noble kings. This caused Yan Wang Zhu Di (燕王朱棣) to uprising. He led his troop attack into the capital, Ying Tainfu, and became the emperor. He was Ming Chengzu. Hui Di burnt the palace and killed himself. [16]

Sanbo eunuch went to the south ocean (三保太监下西洋) Zheng He (郑和) was a native of Yunnan, was a Muslim. His nickname was Sanbo (三保). He was a trusted eunuch of Chengzu. In June 1405 AD, Chengzu sent Zheng He to visited nations in southern Asia, with over 200 ships and 27 thousand people. They visited Java, Sumatra, Ceylon, etc. He gave Chengzu's letter and gifts to local kings, established friendship. Close to 30 years, Zheng He went to the south Asian by sea 7 times. The last one was in 1433 AD. He reached Ligudousuo (李骨都索) (now Somalia). [16]

Battle at Tumubao (土木堡之战) Chengzu trusted eunuch more than his officials. Xuanzong (宣宗) and Yingzong (英宗) were the same. Later, the power fell into the hand of a eunuch, Wang Zhen (王振). He was a local rascal. At this time, Wala tribe (瓦剌部) of the Mongolia became stronger.

In 1449 AD, Wala confronted with Ming Dynasty. The confrontation was close to Wang Zhen' s hometown. He wanted to protect his property at his hometown, and he encouraged Yinzong to lead army to fight by himself. Yingzong led 500 thousand men from Beijing to fight but failed. He was captured at Tumubao (now Hailai southeast, Hebei). Yingzong's brother Daizong (代宗) took the throne at Beijing.

Yu Qian (于谦) After Daizong became the emperor, the head of the Military Affairs Yu Qian was responsible for Beijing's defense. Yu Qian respected Wen Tianxiang and was a righteous man. Wala came to attack Beijing. After 5 days battle, Wala was defeated. Yu Qian made a great accomplishment. Seven years later, Daizong was sick. Some old officials supported Yingzong to retake the throne. They hated Yu Qian, because he criticized them before. Out of revenge, they killed Yu Qian.

Qi Jiguang (戚继光) Ming Shizong (明世宗) was the 11th emperor of Ming Dynasty. He trusted the evil Prime Minister Yan Song (严嵩). At this time, southeast coastal area was frequently robbed by Wokou (倭寇) (Japanese pirates). Shizong asked Yan Song to handle this issue. Yan Song suggested to pray to the god of sea and Shizong believed his suggestion. Later, an experienced coastal general, Yu Dayou (俞大猷) was sent to Zhejiang. The problem was calmed down. But later, Yu Dayou was involved in other case and was put in jail. Wokou came back again. This time, general Qi Jiguang was sent to fight Wokou. In 1565 AD, army of Yu and Qi badly defeated Wokou, solved the problem of several decades.

Li Shizhen (李时珍) He was a native of Qizhou (蕲州) (now Qichun, Hubei). His father and grandfather were doctors. He went to mountain to pick up herbs when he was a child. He knew the herb medicine well and cared for patients with his father. He also studied many medical books. At that time, doctor's social status was not high. During Shizong's time, he was recommended to work at Royal Hospital. He noticed the Royal Hospital didn't care about medicine. He stayed one year and left. He noticed many old medicine books had mistakes and lacking new medical information. Therefore, he started to write a medical book. He spent 30 years to finish his book, "Bencaogangmu" (本草纲目) (Compendium of Materia Medica). It recorded 1892 medicines and over 10 thousand prescriptions.

Battle at Sarhu (萨尔浒之战) Shizong died, Muzong (穆宗) took the throne. Six years later, Muzong died. Shenzong (神宗) became the emperor. Shenzong was young. Prime Minister Zhang Juzheng (张居正) managed the nation affairs. It helped the nation follow the right track. Ten years later, Zhang Juzheng died. Shenzong managed the nation by himself and the nation was going downhill. At this time, Jurchen (女真族) at northeast became stronger. In 1616 AD, Aixinjueluo Nurhachi (爱新觉罗

努尔哈赤) claimed to be Khan (汗) [king], with national title Jin (Post-Jin). He led 20 thousand soldiers and conquered Fushun (抚顺). Shenzong sent Yang Gao (杨镐) led 90 thousand men to attack Jin. At Sarhu, Ming army was defeated. In 1625 AD, Nurhachi moved capital to Shenyang (沈阳). Post-Jin became the largest problem to Ming Dynasty.

Xu Guangqi (徐光启) He was a native of Shanghai. He was a patriotic scholar. When he was young, at Nanjing, he met an Italian missionary Matteo Ricci (利玛窦). He became interested in western science. Shenzong let Matteo to do missionary work in Beijing. Soon, Xu Guangqi passed the national examination and came to Beijing. He continued to learn from Matteo. He also did translation of western science books. During Shenzong's time, Xu Guangqi did some work in training troop, but not successful. He went back home. After Shenzong died, Guangzong (光宗) became the emperor, but soon he died. Shenzong's grandson, Xizong (熹宗) took the throne. Xu Guangqi came back to Beijing. He suggested to build cannon, but it wasn't accepted. When he was over sixty years old, he returned home and started farming. He wrote a book, "Nong Zheng Quan Shu" (农政全书), recorded various techniques of agriculture.

Donglin Party (东林党) At later part of Shenzong's period, there was an official, Gu Xiancheng (顾宪成), he was a justice person. He offended Shenzong and was removed from his office. He returned to his hometown Wuxi (无锡) (now Wuxi, Jiangsu) and started to give lecture at Donglin Institute. Sometimes, he would comment on politics. Gradually, he became a well-known person and he and his friends were named as people of "Donglin Party". Xizong was an ignorant emperor. He trusted and favored eunuch Wei Zongxian (魏忠贤). Let him in charge of Dongchang (东厂) (a spy agency). Wei Zongxian did many bad things. He killed many high officials supported Donglin Party and took over the power of the nation.

Yuan Chonghuan (袁崇焕) At Xizong's time, Yuan Chonghuan was responsible defend the northeast. He did a good job. Wei Zongxia wanted him to retreat to Hebei. He was against the idea and led over 10 thousand men stayed at Ningyuan (宁远) (now Xingcheng, Liaoning). Nurhachi saw Ming army retreated to Hebei. He led 130 thousand soldiers to attack Ningyuan, but he was defeated by Yuan Chonghuan. Nurhachi was wounded badly and returned to Shenyang. Few days later, he died. His son, Huangtaiji (皇太极) became the Khan. The next year, Huangtaiji came to attack Ningyuan and was also defeated. Wei Zongxia claimed all the success. Soon, Xizong died. His brother Sizong (思宗) (Chongzhen Di (崇祯帝)) took the throne. He knew the evil Wei Zhongxia committed. He demoted him to be a soldier. Wei Zhongxia killed himself. Huangtaiji knew he was not able to defeat Yuan Chonghuan. So he detoured to attack Beijing directly. Yuan Chonghuan led his troop came to rescue. Huantaiji used a counterplot. He let a Ming eunuch to tell Chongzhen Di that Yuan Chonghuan collaborated with Post-Jin against Ming. Chongzhen Di believed this lie. He put Yuan Chonghuan in jail. The next year, Yuan was killed. After this incident, Huangtaiji returned to Shenyang. In 1635 AD, he changed the name of Jurchen to Manchuria (满州). One more year, he claimed to be the king, with the national title Qing (清).

Li Zicheng (李自成) He was a native of Mizhi (米脂) (now Yulin, Shaanxi). His family was peasant. He liked horse riding and archery, good at martial art. He was in charge of collecting tax. One time, there was a peasant could not pay the tax due to famine. He borrowed some money to pay the tax for him, but he was not able to pay back the debt and was put in jail. Someone helped him and he became a soldier. Later, because of an argument, he killed an officer and led people to uprising. He followed Chuang Wang (闯王) Gao Yingxiang (高迎祥). After Gao died, he became the Chuang Wang. Chongzhen Di sent troop to attack them, but they didn't perish, but even more spreaded. In 1644 AD, Li Zicheng established an empire, with national title Dashun (大顺). He led one million people using two routes to attack Beijing. Within 3 months, Beijing fell and Chongzhen Di killed himself by hanging at Meishan (煤山). Ming Dynasty was ended.

Wu Sangui (吴三桂) Li Zicheng entered Beijing. People welcomed him. He strictly punished the corrupted officials. Wu Sangui was the Commander of Shanhaiguan (山海关). He had several 100 thousand soldiers. Li Zicheng persuaded Wu to surrender but failed. Then, he led more than 200 thousand men to attack Shanhaiguan. When Wu knew this, he turned to Qing for help. At this time, the emperor of Qing was Qing Shizu (清世祖), son of Huangtaiji. He was only 6 years old. His uncle, Duoergun (多尔衮), was in charge. Duoergun agreed with Wu Shangui's request and led over 100 thousand soldiers to help. When two armies fought, Li Zicheng was defeated. He went to Xian and was killed. In October 1644 AD, Qing Shizu Shunzhi Di (顺治帝) entered Beijing, started Qing Dynasty.

Shi Kefa (史可法) After Chongzhen Di killed himself at Meishan, Fu Wang (福王) took the throne at Nanjing. It was South Ming (南明). Fu Wang was ignorant, only knew enjoying life. At that time, there were 4 armies at north of Yangtze River, but they fought and disagreed with each other. Shi Kefa was Minister of Military. He requested to go to the front line. After he arrived at Yangzhou, he went to talk to the generals, persuaded them not to fight each other. Soon, Duoduo (多铎) led Qing army came south. Shi Kefa died in the battle of Yangzhou. Few days later,

Qing conquered Nanjing and finished the ruling of Fu Wang.

Zheng Chenggong (郑成功) After Yangzhou fell, Qing continued moving south, all the way to Jiading (嘉定). In June, Huang Daozhou (黄道周) and Zheng Zhilong (郑芝龙) helped Tang Wang (唐王) to be the emperor at Fuzhou (福州), started another South Ming Dynasty. Zheng Zhilong had the military power. He was not interested to fight. One year later, he surrendered to Qing and finished the ruling of Tang Wang. His son, Zheng Chenggong didn't agree with his father's decision. He severed the relationship with his father and built a navy at Xiamen (厦门). At this time, Gui Wang (桂王) became the emperor at Guangxi (广西). He named Zheng Chenggong as the Grand General to fight northward. Zheng led 170 thousand navy advanced into Yangtze River. He attacked Nanjing used water and land routes but failed. He retreated to Xiamen. At this time, Qing occupied most Fujian (福建). They adopted a blockade policy, planned to cut off Zheng's supply. Zheng decided to expand to Taiwan. In April 1661 AD, Zheng Chenggong led 25 thousand men, serval hundred warships, leaving Jinmen (金门) drove away the Dutch from Taiwan. In 1662 AD, Zheng Chenggong died, his son Zheng Jing (郑经) took over and continued fighting against Qing. In 1680 AD, Zheng Jing died, his son Zheng Keshuang (郑克塽) took over. In 1683 AD (the 22nd year of Kangxi (康熙)), Zheng Keshuang surrendered to Qing Dynasty, ended the effort of against Qing. [4, 17]

II. Chinese history after Qing dynasty

II.1 Qing Dynasty (清朝) [2, 4] 1644-1911 AD: It had 10 kings, total 268 years.

In 1661, Shunzhi Di died, his son Shengzu (圣祖) (Kangxi Di (康熙帝)) became the emperor. He was only 8 years old. The nation was ruled by 4 high officials. When Kangxi was 14 years old, he ruled the nation by himself. He disciplined the officials, encouraged production, and strictly punished corruption. Qing Dynasty became stronger. In his earlier years of ruling, he used a scheme to kill an authoritarian high official Aobai (鳌拜) to gain power for himself. He ruled the nation 61 years, forced man of Han tribe to wear Qing clothes and pigtail.

Put down three noble kings (平定三藩) When Gui Wang of South Ming was perished, there were three noble kings at the south, very powerful. They were the three surrendered generals of Ming Dynasty, Wu Sangui at Yunnan and Guizhou, Shang Kexi (尚可喜) at Guangdong, and Geng Zhongming (耿仲明) at Fujian. Shang Kexi requested to retire and go home. It was approved by Kangxi, but not allowed his son to continue his position. Wu Sangui and Geng Jinzhong (耿精忠) (grandson of Geng

Zhongming) also requested to release the duty to check the intention of the emperor. Kangxi approved their request also. In 1673, Wu Sangui united the other two noble kings rebelled. Kangxi spent 8 years to put them down.

Jaxa (雅克萨) When Kangxi calmed down the three noble kings' rebel, Russia Czar invaded Jaxa (now Huma northwest, Heilongjiang; northern bank of Heilongjian, east of Mohe). In 1685, Kangxi sent 15 thousand men drove the Russian away. Summer of the next year, Russian came back to occupy Jaxa. Once again, Qing army chased them away. In 1689, China and Russia signed the Nybchu Treaty (尼布楚条约), acknowledged the river basin of Heilongjian and Ussuri River (乌苏里江) belonged to China.

Literary prison (文字狱) Kangxi used official positions to attract the intellectuals of Ming Dynasty to follow him and worked at capital, but there were people not willing to follow. He checked people's writing. If he found someone didn't like his ruling, he would put this person in jail or kill him. This was the literary prison. After Kangxi died, Shizong (世宗) (Yongzheng Di (雍正帝)) became the emperor. More literary prison cases showed up. The purpose was to suppress people's anti-Qing intention.

He Shen (和珅) After Yongzheng died, his son Gaozong (高宗) (Qianlong Di (乾隆帝)) took the throne. He put down the internal rebel, reinforced control of Xingjiang (新疆) and Tibet. When he was old, he trusted a big corrupted official, He Shen. He ruled the nation 60 years. Four years before he died, in 1796, his son Renzong (仁宗) (Jiaqing Di (嘉庆帝)) became the emperor. He sentenced He Shen to die and confiscated his properties. They found He Shen's property worth 800 million liang silver [400 million kg], equivalent to 10 years nation's tax income.

Bailian Teaching (白莲教) During the later period of Qianlong, Qing was going downhill, officials were corrupt, and people had hard time to make living. At Hubei and Henan, Bailian Teaching (白莲教) [Bailian means white lotus.] was prevailed. It said Qing Dynasty was to be ended and a new world was coming, anyone joined the teaching would have land. It attracted many people to join them. The year Jiaqing took the throne, Bailian Teaching revolted at Hubei. Qing Dynasty spent 8 years to put it down. After this incident, Qing Dynasty was weaker.

Opium War (鸦片战争) In 1820, Jiaqing died, Xuanzong (宣宗) (Daoguang Di (道光帝)) became the emperor. At this time, British sold opium to China to make money. In November 1838, Lin Zexu (林则徐) as an Emperor's Envoy (钦差大臣) went to Guangzhou to investigate the damages caused by opium. Next year, Lin Zexu confiscated the opium from the British merchants, total 1420 tons, burnt at the beach of Humen (

虎门). In June 1840, British sent warships to attack Guangzhou, but they were defeated by Lin Zexu. British went northward. They took Dinghai (定海), straight to Tianjin (天津). In August 1842, British forced Qing Dynasty to sign the 1st unequal treaty, Nanjing Treaty (南京条约) [19]. Lin Zexu was removed from duty. The next year, British forced Qing Dynasty to sign Five-port Trade Regulatons (五口通商章程) and Humen Treaty (虎门条约). [19] In 1844, USA and France forced Qing Dynasty to sign an unequal treaty separately, Wangxia Treaty (望夏条约) and Huangpu Treaty (黄埔条约). [19] [1997, British returned Hong Kong to China.]

Taiping Hevenly Kingdom (太平天国) Hong Xiuquan (洪秀全) was a native of Hua (花县), Guangdong. His family were peasant. He was an intellectual. He participated the examination 4 times but failed. Later, he read a book "Quan shi liang yan" (劝世良言) [Advice to the world] written by a Chinese Christian Liang Fa (梁发). He believed in God, pursuing equality for everyone, but he didn't study Bible and wasn't baptized. In 1847, he founded a religion "Religion of Worship God" at Guiping, Guangxi. He claimed to be the brother of Jesus and started missionary work. In January 1851 (the 2nd year of Wenzong (文宗) (Xianfeng Di (咸丰帝)) after Daoguang died), he revolted against Qing at Jintiancun (金田村), Guiping, Guangxi, with national title Taiping Heavenly Kingdom. He claimed himself to be Tian Wang (天王). In 1853, he conquered Jiangning (江宁) (now Nanjing), changing its name to Tianjing (天京) and kept it as his capital. He set up five Wangs, published "Tianchao Tianmu Zhidu" (天朝田亩制度) [a system of land distribution] to help farmer solve the land problem. [20] At the meantime, he sent troop westward to fight for the midsection of Yangtze River and northward to fight for Beijing. The west route successed, but the north route failed. British sent someone to talk to Hong Xiuquan, requested it to acknowledge its treaties with the Qing Dynasty, but it was rejected by Hong Xiuquan. Therefore, British didn't help him, but the Qing Dynasty. In 1856, internal fighting broke out in Taiping Heavenly Kingdom. Dong Wang (东王) Yang Xiuqing (杨秀清) and his 20 thousand subordinates were killed by Bei Wang (北王) Wei Changhui (韦昌辉). This was the Tianjing incident. Later, Hong Xiuquan killed Wei Changhui and invited Yi Wang (翼王) Shi Dakai (石达开) to manage the nation. But Hong didn't trust Shi. It caused Shi Dakai led his several 10 thousand subordinates to leave Hong. Taiping Hevenly Kingdom was going downhill. In June 1864, Hong Xiuquan died. In July, Taijing fell and Taiping Hevenly Kingdom perished. [18]

The 2nd Opium War (第二次鸦片战争) 12 years after signed Nanjing

Treaty, British misinterpreted Wangxia Treaty and asked to revise Nanjing Treaty, hoping to gain more advantages. It was refused by Qing Dynasty. In 1856, USA requested to revise Wangxia Treaty and it was also rejected. Western powers were ready to start another invasion of China. In the same year, British, using the excuse of the incident of Yarrow (亚罗号事件), and French, using the excuse of French priest Father Ma incident (马神父事件), organized a united army to invade China. They first took Guangzhou. USA and Russia encouraged this invasion and were willing to be the mediator to gain benefits. In May 1858, British and French army reached Tianjin. In June, Qing Dynasty signed Tianjin Treaty with British, French, USA, and Russa. [19] In June 1859, British and French disagreed the location to exchange the Tianjin Treaty (天津条约) and marched their troop to Dagukou (大沽口), but they were defeated by Qing's army. In February 1860, British and French troop (15 thousand British, 7 thousand French) invaded China again. In October, they took Beijing, looting and killing for 50 days. They also burnt Yuanmingyan (圆明园) [royal garden] for 3 days and 3 nights, forced Qing Dynasty to sign Beijing Treaty (北京条约). [18, 19]

Russia invaded China Russia Czar took the advantage that Qing Dynasty was busy dealing the British and French troop; invaded vast land of China. In May 1858, Qing Dynasty and Russia signed Aihun Treaty (瑷珲条约). Russia seized the territory north of Heilongjiang, south of Wai Xinganling (外兴安岭) of over 600 thousand sq. km. The territory east of Ussuri River was changed to co-own by both nations. In 1860, Russia claimed that they made contribution in mediation, forced China to sign Beijing Treaty to give Russia the territory east of Ussuri River, total 400 thousand sq. km. In 1864, Russia forced Qing Dynasty to sign "Kangfeng Xibei Jieyueji" (勘分西北界约记) [A survey of northwest border], giving Russia the territory east and south of Balkhash Lake (巴尔喀什湖), total 440 thousand sq. km. The territory China lost was over 150 thousand sq. km., about three times the area of France. [19]

Empress Dowager Cixi (慈禧太后) In 1861, Xianfeng died, Muzong (穆宗) (Tongzhi Di (同治帝)) became the emperor. He was only 5 years old. Per Xianfeng's will, 8 high officials would help him run the nation, but later, Tongzhi's mother, Empress Dowager Cixi, launched a coup, seized the power. [18]

Westernization movement It is also called Tongzhi Modernization (同治维新). The humiliation of Qing Dynasty at the international made some officials advocate to learn from the west, their advance technique, to make China strong and rich. This was the movement of westernization. They built military industry, civil industry, navy, new school, sent students to study overseas, etc. But because of the corruption of Qing Dynasty, it didn't save Qing Dynasty. [18]

Sino-French War At the end of 1883, French attacked Qing's army in Vietnam. French was defeated. But Qing Dynasty signed another unequal treaty with France, like a defeated nation. [18]

Zuo Zhongtang protected Xinjiang (左宗棠) In 1867, a Tajik native (塔吉克人) Yakub (阿古柏), under the encouragement of Czar and British, invaded Xinjiang and set up a government there. In 1871, Russia invaded and took Yili (伊犁), cooperated with Yakub. At end of 1875, head of Shaanxi and Gansu (陕甘総督) Zuo Zhongtang drove them away, protected Xinjiang. In 1881, Sino-Russian Yili Treaty was signed. [18, 19]

Sino-Japanese Jiawu War (中日甲午战争) In 1894, Joseon Dynasty (朝鲜王朝) had internal unrest. Japan used it as an excuse sent troop to Korea. Japan also attacked Liao peninsula in China. At Lushun, Japan massacred people for 4 days and 3 nights, killed 20 thousand people. Chinese Beiyang Navy (北洋水师) fought fiercely but was defeated due to lack of ammunition (Its money was used to build Summer Palace (颐和园) for Empress Dowager Cixi.). In 1895, Qing Dynasty and Japan signed Shimonoseki Treaty (马关条约). [18, 19]

Wuxu Coup (戊戌政变) In 1874, Tongzhi died, Dezong (德宗) Guangxu Di (光绪帝) became the emperor. He was only 4 years old. Empress Dowager Cixi was in power for the 2nd time. When Guangxu was in charge, he advocated modernization. In June 1898, he started to change the government, but only 100 days. It was stopped by Empress Dowager Cixi. Guangxu was put in house arrest until he died. [18]

Boxer Rebellion (义和团事变) Because foreign power's invasion of China, plus the difficult life for the Chinese people, it caused the boxer rebellion against foreigners in China. Boxer was an organization in Shandong and Hebei to teach people martial arts. In 1899, boxer launched a nationwide anti-foreign movement. Many foreigners were killed. It caused the united army from 8 nations (British, France, USA, Russia, Japan, Germany, Italy, Austria) to attacked China. They entered Beijing. In 1901, Qing Dynasty signed Xinchou Treaty (辛丑条约). [18, 19] 1900, Russia Czar took advantage of the Boxer Rebellion, invaded China's Jiangdong Sixty-four area (3600 sq. km, north of Heilongjiang River), slaughter local people and occupied the land. [19]

Sun Zhongshan (孙中山) [Sun Yatsen] His name was Sun Wen (原名孙文). He was a native of Guangdong, a Christian, a doctor, and a great patriotic revolution leader. In 1894, he founded Zongxinghui (中兴会) to promote people to overthrow Qing Dynasty. In 1905, he united other revolutionary organizations and organized Tongmenghui (同盟会). After 12 times uprising, on October 10, 1911, uprising at Wuchang was a successful one. It also called Xinhai Revolution (辛亥革命). The whole nation responded. On February 2, 1912, emperor of Qing Dynasty resigned and Republic of China started. [18, 21]

II.2 Republic of China 1911 to now. [18, 21]

On January 1, 1912, Sun Yatsen took the position as the Provisional President. Considering the situation of the nation, Sun decided to concede his position to Yuan Shikai (袁世凯), because Yuan controlled the military forces in the north. Yuan Shikai moved the capital to Beijing. In August, Tongmenghui revised its name to Kuomingtang (国民党). In March 1912, in order to gain power, Yuan Shikai assassinated Song Jiaoren (宋教仁) who was the leader of Kuomingtang. In March 1913, Sun Yatsen launched the 2nd revolution against Yuan Shikai but failed. In October, Yuan became the president. In January 1915, Japan requested the 21 items to perish China (日本 21 条灭亡中国的要求) to Yuan Shikai. In May, Yuan Shikai accepted the request. [22] In December, Yuan Shikai claimed to be the emperor, but he was opposed widely. In March 1916, he cancelled his emperor position. In June, Yuan died. At Guangzhou, Sun Yatsen ready to launch the 3rd revolution (the North Expedition).

May Fourth Movement (五四运动) On May 4, 1919, 3 thousand Beijing students marched to protest: the 21 items Japan planned to add to China and foreign power plan to transfer of right of Shandong from German to Japan. During World War I (WWI), China sent civil workers to help fighting in Europe, but after the war, at the Paris peace meeting, Poland suggested to transfer Germany's right at Shandong to Japan. This incident let us know a weak nation will be bullied and there is no justice in the world. The whole nation supported this patriotic protest. The results: released the arrested students; China refused to sign on the Paris Peace Agreement; abolished the Japan's 21 items request to China; removed three pro-Japan officials (Cao, Zhang, Lu) from their position. Other influence of this movement: patriotic, against imperialism, promotion of science, democracy, and vernacular. [23]

Kuomingtang's North Expedition In July 1921, Chinese Communist Party was established. Sun Yatsen accepted Chinese Communist and united with Russia. It started the 1st cooperation between Kuomingtang and the Chinese Communist. In 1926, Chiang Kaishek (蒋介石) led National Revolutionary Army (国民革命军) for the North Expedition. In 1928, he finished the North Expedition and united China.

The 1st civil war between Kuomintang and Communist During North

Expedition, Communist was expanded in the south. Chiang Kaishek could not tolerate Communist. Therefore, after the North Expedition, he attacked the Communist. After 5 times of attack, in October 1934, Communist started its 250 thousand li long march, moving to Shaaxi, to continue its expansion.

918 Incident British and USA interfered Japan's invasion of China. Japan decided to take Manchuria (China's northest) first. In June 1928, Japanese army assassinated the northern military warlord Zhang Zuolin (张作霖) by exploding his train. Six months later, Zhang's son Zhang Xueliang (张学良) claimed loyal to the central government. It concluded the North Expedition of Kuomingtang. On September 18, 1931, Japanese army attacked Manchuria. Chiang Kaishek ordered Zhang Xueliang not to fight. It caused the fell of Manchuria. In fact, Chinese army had 165 thousand men at the northeast, while Japanese army only had 20 thousand men. [24]

Xian Incident In December 1936, General Zhang Xueliang and Yang Hucheng (杨虎城) arrested Chiang Kaishek at Xian, forced Chiang to stop the civil war and united against Japan. [24]

July Seven Incident (Lugouqiao (卢沟桥) Incident) At 11 PM, on July 7, 1937, Japanese army used an excuse that they lost a soldier at the Lugo Bridge, outside the Wanping County (宛平县), demanding to search the county. It was refused by Colonel Ji Xingwen (吉星文). It was still under negotiation. Japanese army attacked the Wanping County. It started the 8 years of fighting against Japan. Soon, 813 battle at Shanghai started. Chinese army fought bravely against Japanese army. Other fightings during the war, see reference [25].

Nanjing Massacre In November 1937, Shanghai fell. On December 13, Nanjing fell. Within 6 weeks, Japanese army killed people and raped women in Nanjing. 340 thousand Chinese died. This was the Nanjing Massacre. [26]

Fighting against Japan In October 1937, national government moved capital to Chongqiang (重庆). Military factories were successfully moved to Sichuan or other safe locations. It was a great help for continuing fighting against Japan. National government's army fought against Japanese army at the front, while the communist army fought guerrilla war at central and northern China. Lots Japanese army was stucked in China. Communist also implemented land reform and people movement, won the heart of local people. From 1937-1941, Soviet Union assisted national government to fight against Japan, because it was afraid of Japan's invasion of itself. In December 1941, Japan sneak attacked Peral Harbor. It caused USA to declare war against Japan and its assistance to national government to fight Japan. Japanese army also fought into southeast Asia.

In April 1942, China dispatched 100 thousand expedition army into Burma to help British fight against Japan. They won two battles and saved over 7 thousand British soldiers. But British later decided to retreat to India. In April 1944, China sent an expedition (缅甸远征军) to Burma the 2nd time, heavily damaged Japanese army, recovered 130 thousand sq. km land. Dianxi [west of Yunnan] Expedition (滇西远征军) also recovered 38 thousand sq. km land at west of Yunnan. [27] From April to June 1945, Japan launched the last attack in China, the battle of Xiangxi (湘西) [west of Jiangxi] and was defeated. Then, Japan was at its defensive position.

Surrender of Japan June 1942, Japanese navy was defeated at Midway Island by American. Later, Japanese army's power at pacific and south China sea were faded. In June 1944, Japan was defeated in the sea battle at Mariana (also called the Battle of the Philipine Sea]. Japan lost the control of the air and American airplanes started to bomb Japan. On August 6, 1945, USA dropped two atomic bombs at Japan. On August 15th, Japan surrendered. It ended WWII.

The 2nd civil war between Kuomingtang and Communist In January 1941, national army attacked the new 4th army of the Communist. It led to the broken cooperation between Kuomingtang and Communist. Purportedly, the national government talked peace to Japan three times during the war. [28] After winning the war against Japan, Chiang Kaishek started attack Communist. Communist was forced to leave Yanan (延安), their home. But soon the battle situation turned around. Communist first took the northeast and the northwest and easily gained the central and northern China, the places where they fought gurellia war before. The national government forces could only control few local cities, while the Communist army controlled bigger rural areas. The Communist army quickly across the Yangtze River and united China. The national government retreated to Taiwan and stayed there until today. On October 1, 1949, the People's Republic of China was founded at Beijing. From March to May 1950, Communist used simple wooden ships defeated contemporary navy of the national government and liberated Hainan (海南岛). In May, they also liberated Zhoushan Islands (舟山群岛) and Wanshan Islands (万山群岛) at the mouth of Peral River (珠江). Communist gained the control of the coastal areas. During the battle at Wanshan Islands, again Communist used few simple warships and defeated the regular navy of the national government.

The independent of Mongolia Starting 1920's, Russia supported the independence of Mongolia. In August 1945, national government signed peace treaty with Soviet Union, agreed to let Mongolia to decide independence by voting. In October, Mogonlia voted to be independent and left China. [29]

II.3 The People's Republic of China 1949 till now. [18]

Suppressed the anti-revolution (镇压反革命运动) From 1950 to January 1951, China developed a movement to suppress the anti-revolution. Main purpose was to consolidate its political power and to remove the remaining forces from the national government, spies, and bandits. Estimated about one million people were killed, some of them were killed by mistakes. [30]

Helped north Korea to fight American (抗美援朝) In October 1950, China sent volunteers to fight American in North Korea. They fought American back to the 38 latitude. In July 1953, the war ended. [30] Because of this war, Soviet Union agreed to help China.

Land reform (土地改革运动) From 1950 to 1953, China implemented land reform, killed about 2-3 million landlords, distributed the land to farmers. It completely eliminated the landlords and consolidated the ruling. [30]

Other political movements From 1951 to 1952, 3-anti and 5-anti movements (三反、五反); from 1953 to 1956, three major transformations (三大改造); 1956, hundred flowers bloom and hundred schools contend (百花齐放，百家争鸣). Many people were wrongly criticized; 1957, anti-rightist campaign (反右派斗争), many intellectuals were wrongly criticized. [30]

Great Leap Forward (大跃进) In May 1958, China implemented the Great Leap Forward movement. It was hoped to rely on the force of the multitude to help nation leap forward. It was a mistake and caused great backward in agriculture and industry. The worse was it caused famine, killed about 20 million people from 1958 to 1962. [30]

People's Commnue (人民公社) At the meantime of the Great Leap Forward, China implemented People's Commnue, encouraging people to join, turned in private land to the public, work together, and eat together. The result didn't improve production. [30]

Culture Revolution (文化大革命) Due to the failure of the Great Leap Forward, the leaders of the Chinese Communist started to revise its course. Mao Zedong (毛泽东) considered this was wrong. In May 1966, he launched Culture Revolution, calling Red Guards to lead all the people to fight against the government and its workers. Because the participants didn't know what was right or wrong, didn't know how to make improvement, but destruction, it caused 10 years disaster. In October 1976, the gang of four were arrested, and the Culture Revolution ended. [30]

Reform and Opening Up (改革开放) In December 1978, Deng Xiaoping (邓小平) became the leader of the Chinese Communist. He adopted the market economic of the capitalism. His theory was 'No matter the cat is white or black. If it can catch mice, it is a good cat.'. He threw away the political theory, emphasized on method to solve practical problems. This was the Reform and Opening Up. Forty years later, China becomes the 2nd largest economic country in the world and still moves forward. [30]

Other development in China In June 1959, Soviet Union withdrew their assistance to China. China started to move ahead by itself. In October 1964, China developed atomic bomb; June 1967, developed Hydrogen bomb; 1968, built Nanjing Yangtze River Bridge; April 1970, launched man-made satellite; June 2006, built Three Gorges Dam; July, Qinghai-Tibet Railroad was opened to the public; September 2016, Tianyan (天眼) was built; October 2018, Hong Kong-Zhuhai-Macao Bridge (港珠澳大桥) was opened to the public. These events tell us that China has talents. China also develops its business, in Africa and Belt and Road Area (一带一路地区).

Protected homeland In June 1962, India invaded Tibet and was defeated by China. In March 1969, Soviet Union invade Zhenbao Island (珍宝岛) and was defeated. In February 1979, Vietnam invaded Guangxi and Yunnan and was defeated. [30]

India invaded Southern Tibet (印度侵佔藏南) When India was British colony, British invaded Lhasa, Tibet in August 1904. British also invaded Southern Tibet, using McMahon line as the border which China never acknowledges. When India became independent, it took Southern Tibet as a province. This area is still an area of controversy. [30]

III. Some thought

From Chinese history, we see people want peace, able to happily live with family. They want a government which is fair and without corruption, able to treat other nations with mutual benefits, equal and justice. People's Republic of China is not perfect, but basically it did what it supposed to do. China doesn't need unrest, but it needs to advance forward and continues improvement.

After China becomes stronger, it doesn't follow the imperialism. It treated other nation equally, with mutual benefits, and doesn't interfere other nation's internal affairs. From Chinese history, we see the sinful nature of human, struggle/glory of justice, ups and downs in history, people's limitation, and people want fair/justics.

IV. God's word [Bible verses from New Testament (Standard version)]
John 3:16-17 For God so loved the world, that he gave his only Son, that whoever believes in him should not perish but have eternal life. For God did not send his Son into the world to condemn the world, but in order that the world might be saved through him.

Mark 16:16 Whoever believes and is baptized will be saved, but whoever does not believe will be condemned.

Notes:
1. Four old civilized nations in the world are China, Egypt, Babylon, and India.
2. Mandarin Daily News Dictionary (国语日报辞典); 1st publication in Dec. 1974; by Mandarin Daily News Publication; Taiwan, China.
3. Story of Yao, Shun, and Yu. See website:
https://wenku.baidu.com/view/1e37d41f227916888486d7f0.html?sxts=1552601172741
4. Up and Down for Five Thousand Years (上下五千年), Vol. 1-5; Editor: 林汉达，曹余章; Published by (Shanghai) Youth Children Publication (少年儿童出版社); Oct. 1979, 1st edition.
5. Zhou's 700 thousand-men army was organized in a hurry. Some were slaves and some were captives of Dongyi, not loyal to Zhou. During fighting many of them defected.
6. Stopping fighting in Chinese is 弭兵.
7. Sun Wu was the author of "The Art of War" (孙子兵法), total 13 Chapters. He was a great military master. He helped Wu Wang Helu defeated Chu. After it, he resigned and lived his own life.
8. Hundred schools of thought (during Spring-Autum and Warring States); Website:https://wenku.baidu.com/view/1d9e1a01ce84b9d528ea81c758f5f61fb7362880.html?from=search
9. During the ceremony of making alliance, ancient Chinese put animal's blood on the lip to show his/her sincerity.
10. The achievements of Wu Di: Policy of "push grace": Noble kings were allowed to give their land to their offsprings. Purpose was to reduce their power; Unified currency: Unified of casting Wuzhu money (五铢钱); Nationalized production of iron and salt: Increased nation's revenue. See website:
https://wenku.baidu.com/view/92217502a6c30c2259019e45.html?rec_flag=default
11. The castration punishment (宫刑) was a cruel punishment in ancient China. It was banned after Sui Wen Di (581-604 AD). See website:
https://zh.wikipedia.org/wiki/宫刑
12. Emperor's relatives on Empress or Empress Dowager side (外戚).
13. Da Sima Da Jiangjun (大司马大将军) was an ancient title of a military officer. Da Sima (大司马) was the highest military officer. Da Jiangjun was a Grand General, the commander of a troop.
14. Cao Lun (蔡伦) making paper; see website:
https://wenku.baidu.com/view/1d2f7b08f705cc17542709f0.html?from=search
15. Introduction of Li Bai (李白); see website"
https://wenku.baidu.com/view/1de9834433687e21af45a9af.html?from=search

16. In the capital, some people said Hui Di didn't died, but escaped. This puzzled Chengzu and became another reason for him to send Zheng He to visit nations in south Asia.

17. Zheng Chenggong (郑成功); see website:

https://baike.baidu.com/item/郑成功/142

18. Modern Chinese history; see website: https://baike.baidu.com/item/中国近代史/6067; https://baike.baidu.com/item/中国近现代史/9583834

19. Unequal treaty in modern Chinese history; see website: https://wenku.baidu.com/view/12e97cea9a89680203d8ce2f0066f5335a81672c.html?from=search

Content of the unequal treaties:

https://wenku.baidu.com/view/12e97cea9a89680203d8ce2f0066f5335a81672c.html?from=search

Nanjing Treaty (南京条约, 1842): China compensated 21 million silver dollars; ceded Hong Kong; opened 5 trading ports: Guangzhou, Xiamen, Fuzhou, Ningbo, Shanghai; import/export tariff require British consent.

Five-port Trade Regulatons (五口通商章程) and **Humen Treaty** (虎门条约, 1843): United Kingdom (UK) has a territorial jurisdiction (ie, British commit crimes in China will be handled by British.) and one-side MFN (most favorable nation) status (ie, enjoy the privileges of other countries in China).

Wangxia Treaty (望夏条约, 1844): Except of compensation and ceded territory, USA enjoys regulations of Nanjing Treaty and its added treaty. American warships can patrol and inspect at trading ports and build hospital or church at the trading ports.

Huangpu Treaty (黄埔条约, **1844**): France has the same privilege as British and USA; French can build cemetary at trading posts.

Tianjin Treaty (天津条约, 1858): (to UK, France, USA) – Set Embassy in Beijing; open 10 more trading ports: Hankou, Jiujiang, Nanjing, etc.; missionaries can do mission work in China; foreigners can travel, do business in China; foreign merchant ships or warships can tavel at Yangtze River and ports; compensated British and Franch army each 2 million liang silver [1 million kg silver], compensated British merchant 2 million liang silver. (to Russia) – has right to trade on the land and coastal ports; missionary work; has a territorial jurisdiction right and one-side MFN status.

Beijing Treaty (北京条约, 1860): (to UK, France) Tianjin Treaty continues to be effective. Open Tianjin as trading port; ceded Kowloon; increasing compensation to British and Franch army each 8 million liang silver.

China and Russia: Aihun Treaty (瑷珲条约, 1858); **Beijing Treaty** (北京条约, 1860); **Kangfeng Xibei Jieyueji** (勘分西北界约记) [A survey of northwest border] (for details, see sect. II.1 Qing Dynasty – Russia invaded China and Tianjin Treaty of this note (to Russia).

Jiangdong Sixty-four Incident: 1900, Russia Czar took advantage of the Boxer Rebellion, invaded China's Jiangdong Sixty-four area (3600 sq. km), slaughter local people and occupied the land. 1991, during the Jiang Zemin era, China gave up the jurisdiction of this land. See website: https://zh.wikipedia.org/wiki/江東六十四屯

Sino-UK Yantai Treaty (中英烟台条约, 1876): Open Yichang, Wuhu, Wenzhou, Guangdong Beihai as trading port; foreign goods are exempt tax at concession area or inland of China; British can investigate Yunnan trading conditions and travel between India and Tibet, etc.

Sino-Russia Yili Treaty (中俄伊犁条约, 1881): China recovers Yili, but territory west of Horgos River belongs to Russia; compensated 9 million rubles to Russia; Russian merchants don't have to pay tax at north/south of Tianshan; reduce transportation tax of Russian merchandise to Jiayuguan to 1/3.

Shimonoseki Treaty (马关条约, 1895): Ceded Liaodong peninsula (bought back later), Taiwan, Penghu Islands; compensated 200 million liang silver; open Shashi, Chongqing, Suzhou, Hangzhou as trading ports; Japan can build factory at ports.

Xinchou Treaty (辛丑条约, 1901): Signed with 11 nations (UK, France, USA. Russia, Japan, Germany, Italy, Austria, Belgium, Netherlands, and Spain). Compensated 450 million liang silver, paid off by 39 years, including interest total 980 million liang silver); punish the officials advocated fighting, prohibit people to against foreigners; remove the cannons at Dagu cannon station; allowed foreigners to station army at Beijing, Tianjin, and Jingshan Railroad; set Dongjiaominxiang (东交民巷) as an Embassy district, foreigner can keep army, Chinese can not live there; change the Office of Prime Minister to Foreign Affairs Minister, the 1st minister office among the six.

20. Taiping Hevenly Kingdom (太平天国) movement; see website: https://baike.baidu.com/item/太平天国运动/472841?fromtitle=%E5%A4%AA%E5%B9%B3%E5%A4%A9%E5%9B%BD%E8%B5%B7%E4%B9%89&fromid=361333

Hong Xiuquan (洪秀全); see website: https://baike.baidu.com/item/洪秀全

Tianchao Tianmu Zhidu(天朝田亩制度); see website: https://baike.baidu.com/item/天朝田亩制度

21. Xinhai Revolution (辛亥革命); see website: https://baike.baidu.com/item/辛亥革命/5560#3_3

22. Japan's 21 items request to perish China (日本 21 条灭亡中国的要求); https://wenku.baidu.com/view/5e13044b4028915f804dc2b6.html?from=search

23. May fourth Movement (五四运动); see website: https://wenku.baidu.com/view/de1198cbba4cf7ec4afe04a1b0717fd5360cb260.html https://wenku.baidu.com/view/c64ce602326c1eb91a37f111f18583d049640f2e.html?from=search

24. 918 Incident (918 事变); see website: https://wenku.baidu.com/view/b9d2f9d36aec0975f46527d3240c844769eaa086.html?from=search https://wenku.baidu.com/view/63fb3627e55c3b3567ec102de2bd960591c6d953

. html?from=search

25. Sino-Japan fightings (中、日会战); see website:
https://wenku.baidu.com/view/8ae2ad1ff6ec4afe04a1b0717fd5360cba1a8d28.html?from=search

26. Nanjing massacre (南京大屠杀); see website:
https://wenku.baidu.com/view/3590db21f90f76c660371a12.html?rec_flag=default&sxts=1560612919214

27. History of China Expedition (远征军); see website:
https://wenku.baidu.com/view/65d0a95c0166f5335a8102d276a20029bd64632a.html?from=search

28. Thress secret talk between the Chinese national government and Japan;
see website: https://wenku.baidu.com/view/1a9fccd670fe910ef12d2af90242a8956aecaa1d.html?from=search

29. The independent of Mongolia (外蒙古独立的来龙去脉); see website:
https://wenku.baidu.com/view/f1ec6c8571fe910ef12df889.html?rec_flag=default&sxts=1560649720998

30. Suppressed the anti-revolution (镇压反革命运动); see website:
https://baike.baidu.com/item/镇压反革命运动

Helped north Korea to fight American (抗美援朝); see website:
https://baike.baidu.com/item/抗美援朝/383

Land reform (土地改革运动); https://zh.wikipedia.org/wiki/土地改革运动

3 anti and 5 anti movements (三反、五反); see website:
https://wenku.baidu.com/view/5a3e8672542707221 92e453610661ed9ad5155f1.html?rec_flag=default&sxts=1560689481482

Great Leap Forward (大跃进); see website:
https://wenku.baidu.com/view/33140b9f01f69e3142329407.html?from=search

People's Commnue (人民公社); see website:
https://wenku.baidu.com/view/02246a5758fb770bf78a55db.html

Culture Revolution (文化大革命); https://baike.baidu.com/item/文化大革命

Gaige Kaifang (改革开放); https://baike.baidu.com/item/改革开放

Sino-Soviet split (中苏交恶); https://baike.baidu.com/item/中苏交恶

Sino-India War (中印战争); https://baike.baidu.com/item/中印战争

Sino-Vietnam War (对越自卫反击战); see website:
https://wenku.baidu.com/view/f5e1be05f11dc281e53a580216fc700abb6852dd.html?from=search

South Tibet problem (藏南问题); see website:
https://wenku.baidu.com/view/e497511514791711cc79178c.html?from=search
https://wenku.baidu.com/view/5a24197686c24028915f804d2b160b4e767f81bf.html?from=search
https://wenku.baidu.com/view/ead9484ec381e53a580216fc700abb68a982ad8d.html?from=search

Chapter 4 American History

After World War II (WWII), United States of America (USA/America) become the strongest nation in the world. In this chapter, we will introduce the history of America to let us understand this nation better.

I. America before European immigrant came

In 1492, Italian Columbus discovered America in his voyage. Before European immigrated to America, many Indian tribes lived in America.

II. America after European immigrant came [1]

America's land and resources attracted European to immigrate to America. From 17th century, many Europeans started to immigrate to America. They came mainly for the reason of economic and living, to make new life, but some came for the reason of religion, political freedom, or to escape war. Before 1680, most immigrant came from Spain, England, France, and Netherlands. Later, immigrant came from everywhere in Europe. In 1690, British colony at America had 250 thousand people. Later, every 25 years, the population doubled. In 1775, the population reached over 2.5 million people. British colony at America was the 13 areas distributed along the coast of Atlantic Ocean. They used English as their language. They also followed English law and custom. Colony was far away from England. Local people participated local affairs, having the right to rule by themselves. They also had freedom of speech.

The British colony at America, in general, could be divided to three districts. In the north, industry and business were more developed, especially the ship building business. In the middle, land was fertile. Food was the main production. In the south, there were many plantations, produced lots tobacco and cotton, used many blacks.

III. The independence of America

During 1756 to 1763, England/Prussia and the alliance of France/Austria/Spain fought for 7 years. They also fought in America. At the end, England won the war. British took Canada and the land at both side of the upstream of the Mississippi River from France and Florida from Spain.

Background of America independence

King of England hoped to gain profit from its colony at America, but people at the colony hoped to manage their own affairs. British hoped to develop new gained territory slowly, to avoid agitating the Indians, but the people at colony hoped to develop the new gained territory as soon as possible. There was contradiction between them. In 1764, the British collected tax at its America colony, but faced local opposition. The reason was they didn't have representatives at the Parliament. In 1770, British Parliament abolished all the tax except the tea tax at its America colony. In 1773, British allowed East India Company to monopoly the tea trading at the colony. It was opposed by the local merchants. In December, there were 3 East India Company ships at Boston. People threw the tea on the ships into the sea. British started to suppress the rebellion of its colony. In September 1774, representatives from the colony met at Philadelphia for the 1st Continental Congress meeting, discussing how to deal with the British. It was decided to against the British's punishment for Boston and not to trade with British. It also set up "Association" to carry out the resolution. But the British King, George III, didn't want to negotiate with the colony, but demanding obedience. This forced the moderates to join the anti-British movement. In April 1775, British army went to Concord to confiscate people's weapon and arrest rebellion leaders. At village of Lexington, they fought against the local military soldiers. This was the beginning of the American Independent War. Later, British army continued fighting with the local military soldiers, all the way back to Boston. In May, colony representatives met again at Philadelphia for the 2nd Continental Congress. It commanded George Washington as the commander of its civil army to fight for the freedom. In August, King of British acknowledged the rebellion at its America colony. Five months later, Thomas Paine wrote a 50-page pamphlet "Common Sense" to advocate the independence movement.

Declaration of Independence In May 1776, the Continental Congress decided to form a new government for the happiness and safety of the people. On July 4, it made the Declaration of Independence: "…all men are created equal; that they are endowed by their Creator with certain unalienable rights; that among these are life, liberty, and the pursuit of happiness. That to secure these rights, government is instituted among men, …" America was born.

The Independence War Soon after the Declaration of Independence was announced, British army of 30 thousand soldiers took New York, but Washington successful defeated a troop of 18 thousand men. At the end of the year, Washington won the war at Trenton and Princeton. September 1777, British army took Philadelphia and the Continental Congress was forced to flee. At the meantime, the British army from Canada was defeated by American at Vermont. France started to help America more actively. In 1778, due to the threaten from the French warships, British army retreated from Philadelphia. Soon after the winter of 1780, French King Louis 14 sent 6 thousand expedition to help the fighting. French navy interfered the British supply and backup force transportation. At the south, at the beginning of 1780, British occupied Charleston and the whole

Carolinas, but soon, the united force of America and French of 15 thousand men trapped the British army of 8 thousand at Yorktown, at the coast of Virginia. In October 1781, the British army surrendered. British ceased fighting and acknowledged the independence of America. During April to November 1782, both sided started to negotiate. A treaty was signed the next year; British acknowledged the independence of the 13 states of America, the USA (United States of America). America had the territory east of the Mississppi River from British, excepted Florida (which British returned to Spain).

IV. The expansion of USA
IV.1 Before WWI [1, 3]

In May 1787, USA had its Federal Convention at Philadelphia, decided the work of government and each state, a government with three branches (Legislative, Executive, and Judicial), the power of the president, and the Constitution. Soon, Washington was elected as the 1st President. He took the office in April 1789. During this time, the main activity of USA was for people to move westward.

Louisiana Purchase In 1801, Thomas Jeffreson was elected as the President. In 1803, he didn't get the approval of the Congress, he purchased the territory west of Mississippi from Napoleon, total over 1 million sq. mile, for 15 million dollars. This doubled USA's territory. In 1805, Jefferson was re-elected to be the President. During the war between British and French, he took the stand of neutral. But USA ships were detained by both sides and the trade of USA was declined. British detained many Americans in the name of inspection. Jefferson asked Congress to stop trade with other nations, but it made the economic of USA even worse. Later, it was changed to stop trade with the British only.

The 2nd war between USA and British In 1809, James Madison was elected as the President. The relationship between British and USA became worse. In 1812, USA declared war against British. Both sides had win and loss. In 1815, both sides signed Ghent Treaty to end this war. Neither side gained nor lost anything. For USA, over 50 thousand people died; lost 14 hundred ships and many properties. But the sense of a nation was increased. It was the 2nd independent war. It also raised USA's international reputation.

Rebuild after the war After the war, USA started to rebuild; raised tariff to protect its industry; built highway, canals; continued westward development and set up new state governments. The agriculture development of southern states demanded lots black slaves, but not the northern states, who advocated to abolish the slave system.

Florida Purchase In 1819, USA bought Florida from Spain and its right at Oregon, with 5 million dollars.

Monroe Doctrine In 1817, James Monroe was elected to be the President. At this time, European colonies at Latin America also hoped to be independent. USA supported them and recognized their government. In 1822, USA recognized Columbia, Chile, Mexico, and Brazil. In Europe, some nations organized "the Holy Alliance", hoping to protect the power of monarch and suppress the revolution of people. In December 1823, President Monroe made a speech in Congress, against the threat of Europe. This was the Monroe Doctrine. His main points were: 1. Europe nations should not treat independent nations in America as their colony. 2. If Europe nations pushed their system to any place in the world, it would be a threat to our peace and safety. 3. USA would not interfere the colonies of European nations. 4. USA would not join the war among the European nations.

War between Mexico and USA In 1821, Mexico became independent from Spain. In 1836, Texas was independent from Mexico; in 1845, Texas joined USA. From 1846 to 1848, USA and Mexico fought against each other. Mexico was defeated. In February 1848, two nations signed Guadalupe Hidalgo Treaty. USA gained California, Utah, Navada, Arizona, and part of Colorado and New Mexico, a vast territory. In 1854, through Gadsden Purchase, USA gained Arizona and south New Mexico, a territory of 29670 sq. mile; the cost was 10 million dollars. [2]

Gold in California In January 1848, gold mine was found in California. People from everywhere in the world came to California to find gold. In 1849, 80 thousand people rushed into California.

Other activities Labors started to organize. In 1836, union members reached 300 thousand at north coastal area. Labors received better working conditions. Free education system was set up in each state. Women started to join the women movement to raise their right. Many literatures appeared also. Writer Emerson advocated individualism and human dignity. From 1825 ti 1850, people's life greatly improved; wheat threshing machine, reaper, and lawn mower were invented; railroad was continuously deve- loped. In 1835, Morse invented electric telegraph. In 1847, Richard Hoe designed the rotary printing press, making revolutionary progress for the publication business. From 1812 to 1852, USA population increased from 7.25 million to 23 million, territory increased from 1.7 million sq. mile to 3 million sq. mile, about the same size as Europe. USA had 31 states.

Civil War Most southern USA were farms, while most northern USA were cities. People in these two places had different thought, especially about slavery. Northerner advocated to abolish it, while the southerner wanted to keep it. This contradiction led to Civil War. In 1860, Abraham Lincoln was elected as the President. In February 1861, the southern states founded the Confederate States of America, left USA. In March, Lincoln took office. He refused to recognize the Confederate. In April, Confederate fired at

Fort Sumter, a fortress at Charleston, South Carolina. It started the Civil War. The north (Union) had 23 states, 22 million people; the south (Confederate) had 11 states, 9 million people. The north had better industry than the south.

The Civil War was fought in three areas: 1. At sea: Uion's navy was superior. It successfully stopped the trade between Confederate and Europe. 2. At Mississppi River: General Grant successfully took the area along the river, forced Confederate to be divided into two parts. 3. At eastern coastal states: At the beginning, Uion's army was defeated by Confederate's General Lee. But after July 1863, the battle situation was reversed. In April 1865, Confederate army surrendered. It ended the Civil War.

In January 1863, Lincoln announced the Emancipation Proclamation; announced abolishing the slavery system.

Assassination of Lincoln In 1864, Lincoln was re-elected to be the President. In April 1865, 5 days after the surrender of the Confederate, Lincoln was assassinated. Lincoln advocated to be lenient to the southern states. In his 2nd term inaugural speech, he said: "…With malice toward none; with charity for all, with firmness in the right, as God gives us to see the right, …to do all which may achieve and cherish a just and lasting peace among ourselves and with all nations."

Rebult after Civil War After Civil War, Congress took the job to rebuild USA, continued protecting black people's civil right. After 12 years effort, in 1877, the whole nation was stabilized.

Alaska Purchase In March 1867, USA bought Alaska from Russia Czar for 7.2 million dollars. In January 1959, Alaska became one state of USA.

The growth and reform of USA From Civil War to WWI, USA made big progress. Industry was developed; the West was developed; agriculture was mechanized; USA became a strong nation. Among them, the development of the West had big impact to the nation. In 1862, per law, everyone would receive 160 acres land, if he/she lived at or used the land. Many people went to the West to do mining, farming, or raising livestock.

During this period, there were many inventions in USA. In 1876, Bell invented telephone; in 1886, Mergenthaler invented a mechanical typeset-ting machine; in 1880, Edison invented light bulb, phonograph, and motion picture; in December 1903, Wright brothers invented the 1st airplane.

During this period, there were many reforms in USA as well. In January 1883, Congress passed the Civil Service Reform Act, improved government's civil service system. Many big companies started to monopolize their business. In 1884, Grover Clevend was elected as the President. In 1887, he approved the Interstate Commerce Act to prevent the unreasonable trading. In 1890, Congress passed Sherman Antitrust Act to prevent the monopoly of big company. In September 1901, President Mckinley was assassinated. Theodore Roosevelt became the President. He did two things during his term: he carried out the antitrust law and protected nation's resources. In 1904, he was re-elected as the President.

Chinese Exclusion Act In May 1882, USA passed the Chinese Exclusion Act; for ten year, no Chinese labor immigrants would be accepted and would not acknowledged non-USA born Chinese offsprings. In 1892, USA passed the harsh Gilari method to expel Chinese. In May 1905, it passed new Chinese exclusion laws, step up prosecution of oversea Chinese. In February 1917, it passed laws to exclude all the Asian immigrants.

War between USA and Spain In 1895, anti-Spain revolution happened in Cuba. In February 1898, America warship Maine was destroyed at Havana harbor, causing 260 people died. In April, USA declared war against Spain. It only fought 4 months. Spain was defeated. Spain's fleet at Philipines were destroyed and its navy at Cuba was perished. In December, a treaty was signed. Spain ceded Puerto and Guam to USA, USA gained Philipines for 20 million dollars, and Cuba became independent.

Hawaii Hawaii was an independent kingdom before 1893. In 1894, it became a republic. In 1898, it became USA's territory. In 1959, it became a state of USA.

Open Door Policy In 1899, USA suggested Open Door Policy to let China became an open market for the nations to loot.

Big earthquake in San Francisco In April 1912, San Francisco had 7.9 Richter scale earthquake. Fire burnt in the city for few days. Three thousand people died and 80% of the city was destroyed.

Federal Reserve Bank In 1912, Woodrow Wilson became the President. In December 1913, He helped Federal Reserve Bank to be set up at 12 districts in the nation. They were the bank of the banks.

IV.2 Before WWII [1,3]

USA joined the WWI In 1914, WWI broke out in Europe. At the beginning, USA didn't join the war. But later, German submarine sinked 5 America merchant ships. In April 1917, USA joined the war. In October 1918, American army in France had over 1.75 million men. USA helped Allies to win war at sea and at land. In January 1918, President Wilson set out 14 Points for peace. He also suggested to establish an international league to maintain the peace in the world. In 1918, Germany was defeated and asking for peace. In November, the truce agreement was set. In 1919, Congress didn't approve USA to join the League of Nations.

Lansing-Ishii Agreement In November 1917, USA and Japan reached an agreement: USA acknowledged Janpan's privilege in Shandong, Manchuria, and inner Mongolia of China.

The Great Depression After WWI, USA went a conservative and lonely road. It raised tariff to protect its industry; gradually closed the trade with the world. In 1924, Congress passed a law, limited immigrants to 150 thousand people annually. Due to the production exceeded people's buying power, money spent in stock market and real estates, mad investment, in the fall of 1929, it caused the collapse of the stock market. Thousands people lost their saving, stores were closed, factories shut down, banks closed, millions of people lost their job. This was the Great Depression.

The new policy In 1932, Franklin Roosevelt was elected to be the President. He advocated to use the power of government to restore the economy. His new policy quickly carried out and quickly had results. He reformed bank, agriculture, started public works, and helped unemployed workers. He was re-elected twice.

IV.3 WWII

While Roosevelt carried out his new policy, the world situation changed. In September 1931, Japan took Manchuria, started invading China. In 1935-1936, Italiy invaded Ethiopia. In 1938, Germany occupied Austria, continued to invade Czechoslovakia and Lithuania. In September 1939, Germany attacked Poland. The World War II (WWII) started. Germany and Soviet Union splitted and took Poland. In April 1940, Germany invaded Denmark and Norway, in order to protect the safe transportation of iron ore from Sweden. In May, Germany attacked French Maginot Line. Later, it detoured to attack Belgium, Netherlands, and Luxembourg. 340 thousand Allies force abandoned their equipment and safely retreated to England. In June, France fell. In July, Germany started fought against the British air force, but Germany didn't win completely. Germany started to bomb London until May 1941. In November 1939, USA set laws to help China and Allies of Europe, but people didn't want to join the war. [4]

Axis nations September 1940, Germany, Italy, and Japan formed alliance as the Axis nations. In November, Hungary, Slovakia, and Romania joined Axis. In March 1941, Bulgaria and Yugoslavia also joined them.

War at Mediterranean, North Africa, and Balkans In June 1940, Italy attacked British Malta Island at its south, but not able to take it. In fall, Italy took the British Somalia. In September, Italy attacked British Egypt from Libya. In December, Italian army was defeated badly; also lost east part of Libya. In March 1941, allied German force counterattacked from Egypt. It advanced all the way to Tobruk seaport at east of Libya. In November, allied German force was repulsed. In April 1941, allied German force took Greece and Yugoslavia, controlled the whole Balkans. But Yugoslavia people continued to fight against Germany to the end of the war.

Allied German force attacked Soviet Union The contradiction between

Germany and Soviet Union led the Germany attacked Soviet Union in June 1941. In December, allied German force already reached the suburb of Moscow. From August 1942 to February 1943, allied German force and Soviet Union fought the largest war in history at Stalingrad (at south of Soviet Union, now Volgograd). Allied German force was defeated.

Atlantic Treaty In August 1941, UK and USA published the goal of the post-war coalition. Later, it was endorsed by other allied nations and it became the goal for the United Nation. This treaty mentioned following points: not allow to expand territory; people has the right to decide its border; restore the right for a nation to rule by itself; reduce trade limitations; work for better economy and society; no more fear or lack of; freedom at sea; no more attack by force; disarm the aggressor.

Fighting at Asia and Pacific Ocean At the beginning of 1940, China started to counterattack Japan. In August, Chinese Communist started large scale attack at Japan occupied area. In September, Japan cut off the support materials to China from Vietnam; occupied Vietnam and attacked Guangxi. In July 1941, in order to gain more military materials, especially oil, Japan attacked Indochina, threatened the colonies of British and Netherlands. USA frozened Japan's assets and stopped selling oil to Japan. In December 1942, Japan attacked American navy at Pearl Harbor, also attacked Philipines, Thailand, Malaysia, and Hong Kong. Defeated Thailand formed alliance with Japan. In April 1942, Japan occupied Burma, Malaysia, Indonesia, Singapore, and Rabaul (in Papua New Guinea). In May, Japan took Philipines. In April, Chinese Burma Expedition rescued over 7 thousand British soldiers. Japanese won battles at South China Sea, Java Sea, and India Ocean.

Japan was defeated In April 1942, 16 American bombers flied from USS Hornet carrier, bombed Tokyo, Yokohama, and 4 more cities in Honshu. After the bombing, 15 bombers flied to China, crashed. One flied to Soviet Union. Because the bombers were crashed in China, Japan launched Zhejiang-Jiangxi campaign to search the people on the American bombers. Japan spreaded germs of cholera, typhoid, plagues, and dysentery; estimated killed 250 thousand Chinese. In May, Japan fought against the allied force of America and Australia at Coral Sea. Both sides lost greatly of aircraft carriers and airplanes. After this war, allied force started counterattack and Japan lost air superiority. At the end of May, American cracked Japanese navy's code. In June, Japanese navy planned to perish American warships at the Midway Island, but it was known by American. Japan was defeated. In August, American took the islands south of Solomon Islands. Japan counterattacked, but failed. In February 1943, Japan withdrew all its troop there. In May, American and Canadian allied force chased away the Japan army at Aleutian Islands. From November 1943 to February 1944, allied force of USA, Austrilia, and New Zealand took Gilbert and Marshall Islands. In April, allied force started attacking west of New Guinea to the end of the war. From June to November, American attacked Mariana and Palau Islands. In June, while American attacked Mariana Islands, American navy and Japan navy fought a large-scale battle (the Philipines Sea Battle). Japan was badly defeated, lost greatly. After this battle, American built airport at the island and started bombing Japan. In October, American and Austrilian allied force attacked Philipines. At Leyte, a large-scale sea battle happened. Japan used its remaining warships in the battle but was defeated. Japan lost its power to fight at sea. Philippines was completely liberated until the end of the war. In May 1945, Australia recovered Borneo.

Liberation of Burma In March 1944, Japan army attacked India, hoping to take the airport American used to fly supply to China. In June, it was defeated by British and Indian allied force. Then, the allied force counterattacked Burma. In May, Chinese Expedition attacked Japan army at northern Burma. Chinese army took it in August. Opened the Sino-Burma Highway to China. In July 1945, Burma was liberated. From April to June, China counterattacked at Xiangxi. In June, American took Okinawa. In August, American dropped two atomic bombs at Japan. Japan surrendered. In the same month, Soviet Union declared war against Japan, fought into Manchuria.

Allies' meetings In January 1943, USA and UK met at Casablanca (Morocco), decided Axis nations must surrender unconditionally. In November, China, USA, and UK met at Cario (Egypt), decided Japan must surrender unconditionally and abandoned all the gain in the past. In February 1945, USA, UK, and Soviet Union met at Yalta (Crimea), decided after Germany surrendered, Soviet Union to declare war against Japan. In July, USA, UK, and Soviet Union met at Potsdam (Germany), decided the future of Germany and the policy of occupying Germany – to keep its current industry, trial war criminals, compensation to Russia, etc.

European battlefield – at east In August 1942, Allies force took north Africa. In June 1943, Allies started to bomb Germany. In July, German army attacked central Soviet Union, but was pushed back. In the same month, Allies attacked Italy. In June 1944, Allies took Rome. In January 1944, Soviet Union started counterattack. First, it rescued the siege at Leningrad. In May, it took Crimea. In June, it advanced into Belarus, Ukraine, Poland, and Romania. From August to September, Romanian and Bulgaria joined the Allies. In September, it attacked Yugoslavia. In October, it took Belgrade. Then, it advanced into Hungary. In February 1945, it took Budapest. In April, it advanced into east Germany and took Vienna. In the same month, Soviet Union and Poland allied force took Berlin. In May, Germany surrendered.

European battlefield – at west In June 1944, Allies landed at Normandy. In August, Paris was liberated. In December, German army started counterattack, but failed. In April 1945, Allies took Italy and attacked west Germany, joined the army of Soviet Union.

IV.4 After WWII [1, 3]

USA made big contribution for WWII. Its prestige reached its peak in the world. During WWII, American was simple and justice. After WWII, the world was divided to two camps: free democratic nations, headed by USA, and Communism/Socialism nations, headed by Soviet Union. Both camps considered their system was the best. They competed each other in every aspect. This was the cold war. It continues after Soviet Union was disintegrated.

Two mistakes after WWII in Asia 1. USA gave Okinawa to Japan. Okinawa was an independent nation. It was a subordinate nation to China since Ming Dynasty. In 1879, it was annexed by Japan by force. [5] After WWII, according to justice, Okinawa (Ryukyu Islands) should be restored as an independent nation. 2. Diaoyutai Islands belong to China, but they were given to Japan by USA. China never accepts this mistake. From the beginning, national government protested this mistake to USA. It is still an issue unsolved. [6]

USA after WWII After WWII, USA started to reduce its military force, troop from 12 million people reduced to 1.5 million. Government implemented the Servicemen's Readjustment Act (GI Bill of Rights) to help servicemen find a job or continue study. Military industries were converted for civil use. Therefore, no unemployment issue happened. In foreign affairs, USA advocated independence of colonies. In 1946, USA let Philipines to be independent. In 1948, USA and 21 Latin America nations formed Organization of American States to push economic development. In 1949, Truman President advanced his Four Point Program to help develop economic and technical development in the world. In August 1949, USA joined NATO (North Atlantic Treaty Organization), helping defend Europe and north America. In September 1954, USA joined Southeast Asia Treaty Organization to push economic and technical cooperation.

Marshall Plan In June 1947, USA implemented Marshall Plan to help Europe reconstruction. It provided 12 billion dollars to help 16 nations.

Korea War In June 1950, North Korea invaded South Korea. USA led United Nation's forces from 15 nations to counterattack the invasion. It advanced into North Korea. In October, China joined the fight as volunteer fighter pushed United Nation force back to the 38 latitude. In July 1953, an armistice agreement was signed, and North/South Korea were divided by the 38 latitude. In June 1950, the 7th fleet of USA started

To patrol the Taiwan Strait to prevent the attack from China. [7]

Civil Right Movement In 1954, American Supreme Court ruled it was violation of Constitution for black and white to be separated in schools. In February 1960, there was peaceful sit-ins demonstration. It sped up the end of the segregation of restaurants in over 500 southern communities. In 1961, freedom rides demonstration led the Interstate Commerce Commission to ban segregation in all interstate travel. Next year, it was unanimously endorsed by the Supreme Court. Civil Right Movement reached its peak in 1963. In spring, black made a demonstration at Birmingham, south of Alabama. It triggered more demonstration. Soon, President Kennedy presented a legislature to eliminate the racial discrimination in voting, education, employment, and public facilities. In August, 200 thousand people (black and white) gathered at capital Washington DC, made a demonstration, demanding equal rights for people.

Cuba Crisis In October 1962, Cuba allowed Soviet Union to build missile base at Cuba. It was strongly opposed by USA. Later, the missiles were shipped back to Soviet Union.

Vietnam War In July 1954, Geneva Agreement divided Vietnam to North and South Vietnam. France left Vietnam. USA came to help South Vietnam. In 1955, Ngo Dinh Diem under USA support seized the power. In 1959, Viet Gong started guerrilla war in South Vietnam. In May 1961, USA sent 100 special combat men came to South Vietnam. American's Vietnam War started. In November 1963, USA plotted a coup, killed Ngo Dinh Diem. Yan Wenming came to power. In August 1964, USA made an excuse of the Gulf of Tonkin Incident, bombarded North Vietnam. In August 1965, USA army destroyed Viet Cong's base at Van Tuong. In November, USA and North Vietnam fought at Ia Drang fiercely. Neither side won nor lost. After this battle, North Vietnam avoided to fight directly with American. At year end, USA had 184 thousand men in Vietnam. In August 1966, it reached 429 thousand. In 1967, it reache over 500 thousand.

In January 1968, North Vietnam launched Tet Offensive. 80 thousand people attacked every communities in South Vietnam. It caused large destruction. In March, USA planned to withdraw its troop from Vietnam. At this time, anti-war demonstration in USA grew larger and larger. In 1969, President Nixon started withdrew American troop from Vietnam to let South Vietnam to defend itself. In January 1973, Paris Peace Agreement was signed. USA withdrew troop from Vietnam. It ended the 12 years war. In fact, USA still kept many troops in Vietnam to help the 1.1 million Sout Vietnam soldiers to fight. In spring of 1975, North Vietnam and Viet Cong defeated the army of South Vietnam. South Vietnam was perished. In July 1976, Vietnam was unified. [8]

China and USA restored diplomatic relations USA spent lots money, efforts, and materials in Vietnam War, while its opponent, Soviet Union became stronger. Because of this reason, USA started to restore the diplomatic relations with China to balance the power in the world. In January 1979, China and USA restored diplomatic relation.

The Persian Gulf War In August 1990, Iraqi attacked Kuwait. In February 1991, USA, under the agreement of United Nation, led 35 nations' army defeated Iraq, protected the safety of Kuwait and Saudi Arabia. [9]

911 Incident At 9 AM in the morning of September 11, 2001, four airplanes from American northeast area were kidnapped. Two of them flied into the World Trade Center's twin towers in New York, causing them fell down to the ground. Another plane flied to the west side of Pentagon at Washington DC. The last plane was crashed at a village in Pennsylvania. It caused 3 thousand people died, 6 thousand wounded, and property damage over 10 billion dollars. This incident shocked American and the world. In 2004, Muslim leader of Al-Qaida, Osama Bin Laden acknowledged that he planned this attack. The reason was to revenge American's middle east policy and the suppression of Israel to Lebanon and Palestine. In May 2011, USA assassined Bin Laden in Pakistan. [10]

Afhan War After 911 Incident, USA requested Afhan government to hand over Bin Laden. It was refused. In October 2001, USA, British, and Afhan northern alliance attacked Taliban government. In March 2003, Taliban retreated to the south. The northern alliance set up the government. In August 2003, NATO joined to defend Afhan. In 2006, Taliban became stronger again. The foreign troop started to increase. In 2011, there were 140 thousand foreign soldiers in Afhan (100 thousand were American). In 2011, Bin Laden was killed. In December 2014, NATO withdrew its troop. USA also withdrew most of its troop, but not all. In 2017, there were still 13 thousand foreign troop in Afhan. USA still has troop in Afhan. [11]

Iraq War In Marh 2003, USA used an excuse of Iraq owned lots weapons and support the terrorists, attacked Iraq with 130 thousand soldiers. This action didn't have the support or approval of the United Nation. British, Australia, and Poland also sent their troops (45 thousand, 2 thousand, and 2 hundred soldiers respectively) to support the fight. In May, Iraq fell. USA helped Iraqi to set up a democratic government. 2007, USA started to withdraw its troop until 2011. [12]

Syria War In March 2011, Syria civil war broke out. The forces of supporting government, anti-government, and foreign troop fought against each other. This war continues until today. At the beginning, USA was there to support the anti-government force. In September 2014, direct military action was taken. Until now, Russia, Iran, and Hezbolla (of Lebanon) supported the Syria government. USA and Russia didn't confront at each other. [13]

Arms race In July 1945, USA became the 1st nation had atomic bomb. In November 1952, it had Hydrogen bomb (lighter weight and more power than atomic bomb). Soviet Union has atomic bomb in August 1949; hydrogen bomb in August 1953. In July 1955, USA, Soviet Union, UK and France met at Genea for a summit conference, discussed about disarmament issues, but no conclusion. At the beginning, bomber was used to deliver nuclear warhead. From 1950's, missile was adopted. From 1960's, submarine was used also. USA and Soviet Union both knew the power of the nuclear warhead. Dozens of nuclear bombs were enough to destroy the opponent, but either side still kept making nuclear bombs to avoid being behind. Purportedly, the peak of nuclear bombs owner, in 1965, USA had 31 thousand; in 1990, Soviet Union had 40 thousand. In October 1963, USA, Soviet Union, and UK reached an agreement not to do nuclear explosion above the ground and under the water, but it was all right to do it under the ground. Later, 113 nations signed the agreement. In November 1969, USA and Soviet Union started negotiation on SALT (Strategic Arms Limitation Talks). In May 1972, SALT I was signed. It decided each nation could have only two anti-missile bases; each nation to keep its current missiles, not to increase within 5 years. This treaty didn't mention how many warheads each missile could carry. Ten years later, both nations increased their nuclear warheads by 12 thousand. In 1970's, both nations were working on new equipment. In June 1979, both signed SALT II at Genea, limiting each nation's nuclear weapon and technique. But because Soviet Union invaded Afhan in December 1797. USA Congress didn't approve this treaty. In July 1991, USA and Soviet Union signed START I (Strategic Arms Reduction Treaty) at Moscow, to limit a nation's nuclear warheads not over 6 thousand, intercontinental missile and bomber not over 1600. It eliminated 80% of the nuclear weapon. This treaty expired in December 2009. In April 2010, two sides renewed the treaty at Prague as START II. [14]

Race in space In October 1957, Soviet Union launched the 1st man-made satellite. In January 1958, USA also launched its 1st man-made satellite. Race in space started. In July 1969, USA landed on moon, leading the race. From 1972 to 1975, both nations were in cooperation for the work in space. From 1980's, both nations had troop specialized in space military affairs. Aerospace troop became a new type of troop. It started aerospace military competition. The 2003 Iraq War, satellites in space provided many helps to the troop at ground. Who can control the space will control the earth. Therefore, the competition of aerospace military will continue. [15]

Dispute of Sino-USA trade The foreign trade of USA, from 1971 (except 1975) was in red every year and the magnitude was increasing. In 2018, USA claimed the trade deficit between China and USA was 500 billion, intellectual property lost was at 300 billion. USA claimed the trading method of China was unfair. China denied the latter two claims. In China, people think the real reason that USA is making this trade war is to slow the development of China and prevent China ahead of USA. In March, USA raised tariff for 50 billion China goods. In April, China raised tariff for the same value USA goods. In May, both sides did negotiation, but no results. In May, USA raised the tariff on 50 billion China goods to 25%; China did the same to USA. In September, USA raised 10% tariff to 200 billion China goods. China did the same to USA. In December, at the G-20 Summit at Argentina, both sides agreed to stop trade war for 90 days. In January 2019, both sides negotiated again. In May, the negotiation failed. USA raised 25% tariff on 200 billion China goods. China did the same to USA. In June, at the G-20 Summit at Japan, two sides agreed to continue negotiate. China requested USA to be fair to Chinese industries. USA agreed to relax its ban on sale to Huawei. Over one year of this trade war, both had some loss, but not great. China stopped buying soybean from USA and USA trade deficit didn't improve. [16]

Dispute with Iran In April 1979, Iran overthrew the pro-American Pahlavi Dynasty. The relation between Iran and USA worsened. In 1980, Iran and Iraq fought each other. USA first helped Iran, but later, it helped Iraq. In 2001, USA labelled both nations as "Axis of evil". From 1995, USA started embargo to Iran. In 2015, USA led other nations to sign Iran Nuclear Agreement with Iran. In 2016, USA dropped the embargo against Iran. In 2018, USA withdrew from the agreement and started embargo against Iran. In 2019, USA sent warships to Gulf of Persia for the reason of protecting shipping, increased tension in that area. [17]

Hegemonic diplomacy From American history, we see USA shifted from justice to hegemony; from respect God to respect self. USA is a big country, with enough resources and people. It is a big country. The precious things in USA, besides rich, is freedom of speech and religion belief. They will help a nation not to walk in the mistakes. Vietnam war was a good example. American people like individualism, hero, independence, money. After WWII, moral in USA declines, especially the sex relation between men and women. Fortunately, there are still many people know God – believe and know Jesus. USA need more politicians to lead the nation to walk on the road of justice. Hegemony and interfering other nation's internal affairs will not win respect but despise. Any nation in the long term should follow the road God wants us to follow: love/respect others and be justice.

V. God's word [Bible verses from New Testament (ERV)]

Galatians 1:4 Jesus gave himself for our sins to free us from this evil world we live in. This is what God our Father wanted.

Galatians 2:16 But we know that no one is made right with God by following the law. It is trusting in Jesus Christ that makes a person right with God. So we have put our faith in Christ Jesus, because we wanted to be made right with God. And we are right with him because we trusted in Christ - not because we followed the law. I can say this because no one can be made right with God by following the law.

Galatians 5:24-25 Those who belong to Christ Jesus have crucified their sinful self. They have given up their old selfish feelings and the evil things they wanted to do. We get our new life from the Spirit, so we should follow the Spirit.

Notes:

1. American History Outline (美国历史大纲); published by USA Press Office in Taipei, 1966.

2. USA southwestern territory; see website: https://en.wikipedia.org/wiki/Southwestern_United_States#Arrival_of_Europeans

3. Table of American big events in history (美国历史大事年表); https://wenku.baidu.com/view/bd65c179f68a6529647d27284b73f242326c3140.html?from=search

4. World War II; see website: https://en.wikipedia.org/wiki/World_War_II#Italian_invasion_of_Ethiopia_(1935)

5. China Qing Dynasty the canonization of Ryukyu (清代中国对琉球的册封); https://wenku.baidu.com/view/b4cb2621f56527d3240c844769eae009581ba22d.html?from=search

6. Diaoyutai Islands (钓鱼岛争论的由来与现状); see website: https://wenku.baidu.com/view/b74b3fd9dd3383c4bb4cd2a4.html?from=search

7. Korea War (朝鲜战争); see website: https://wenku.baidu.com/view/5d419dc358f5f61fb73666aa.html?from=search

8. Vietnam War; see website: https://en.wikipedia.org/wiki/Vietnam_War ; https://wenku.baidu.com/view/d6c0d6eebdeb19e8b8f67c1cfad6195f312be82e.html?from=search

9. Persian Gulf War; see website: https://en.wikipedia.org/wiki/Gulf_War Why USA launched the Persian Gulf War (探讨美国发动海湾战争的原因); https://wenku.baidu.com/view/2425bedf0b4e767f5bcfce37.html?from=search

10. 911 Incident reason and result (911 事件的原因后果); see website: https://wenku.baidu.com/view/17376e55773231126edb6f1aff00bed5b8f37307.html?from=search ; https://en.wikipedia.org/wiki/September_11_attacks

11. Afghan War; see website: https://en.wikipedia.org/wiki/War_in_Afghanistan_(2001 - present) ;

https://wenku.baidu.com/view/9d918ea2988fcc22bcd126fff705cc1755275faa.html?from=search

12. Iraq War; see website: https://en.wikipedia.org/wiki/2003_invasion_of_Iraq; https://wenku.baidu.com/view/7234bafd0242a8956bece41b.html?sxts=1562951819409

13. Syria War; see website: https://en.wikipedia.org/wiki/Syrian_Civil_War https://en.wikipedia.org/wiki/Americanled_intervention_in_the_Syrian_Civil_War; https://wenku.baidu.com/view/806be65a804d2b160b4ec04c.html?sxts=1563053532327

14. Arms race; see website: https://en.wikipedia.org/wiki/Nuclear_arms_race; https://en.wikipedia.org/wiki/START_I; https://wenku.baidu.com/view/346a57660a4e767f5acfa1c7aa00b52acfc79cc9.html?from=search

15. Space race; see website: https://en.wikipedia.org/wiki/Space_Race; https://wenku.baidu.com/view/bc41ff93c5da50e2524d7fa0.html?sxts=1563466031827

16. Sino-USA trade dispute; see website: https://en.wikipedia.org/wiki/China – United_States_trade_war; https://www.cnbc.com/2019/06/29/us-china-trade-talks-at-g-20-timeline-of-how-the-tariff-war-started.html; https://wenku.baidu.com/view/9fd19e0f30b765ce0508763231126edb6e1a7667.html?from=search

17. Iran dispute; https://en.wikipedia.org/wiki/Iran – United_States_relations; https://wenku.baidu.com/view/b222f603e87101f69e31956e.html?from=search

Chapter 5 Japanese History

In WWII, Japan was an Axis nation. It invaded its Asian neighbors' territory, killed people, burnt houses, raped women, looted property, causing lots damage to its neighbor and hated by people. This chapter Japanese history will be presented to let us understand Japan better.

I. The origin of Japanese

There are 5 possible origins of Japanese: 1. According to the legend of Japan, they are offspring of god. 2. Archaeologist thinks Japanese ancestors came from the continent of Asia before the Ice Age (500 thousand years ago). 3. Anui (Shoji) people lived at northern Japan are white (Caucasian), came from the continent of Europe/Asia. 4. Japan is fertile. Many Korean and some Chinese immigrated to Japan. 5. There was a record in Chinese history: During Qin Dynasty (221-206 BC), Xu Fu (徐福) brought 3 thousand boys and girls to seek the method to live forever. Legend said they arrived Japan. [1]

II. Japanese history [2]
II.1 Ancient time
II.1.1 Earlier stage (9 thousand years ago to 12th century)

Jomon Era: 9 thousand years ago to 4th century BC. People lived by hunting. People already had pottery. The patterns on the pottery mainly were rope. People lived in small groups.

Yayoi Era: 4th century BC to 3rd century AD. During this era, farming was common, and fishery was also developed. People started to use bronze and iron equipment. During 1st to 2nd century AD, many small countries existed. They fought against each other. Later, power fell into the hand of Qeen Himiko of Yamatai.

Yamato Era: 3rd to 6th century AD. Yamato Dynasty ruled Japan. During this era, there were many old tombs, some were quite large. Therefore, this era also called ancient tomb era. Yamato Dynasty had close relation with China. Chinese words, Confucianism, Buddhism, and various skills were introduced into Japan during this era. Japan started having history records. In Chinese history, there was recording about Japan came to China to make tributes.

Asuka Era: From 538 to 710 AD. Prince Shotoku took the throne. He learned the system and culture from Sui Dynasty of China. His reform pushed the advance of Japan. He also advocated Buddhism. His capital was at Asuka. Therefore, it was called Asuka Era. After Shotoku died, Emperor of Japan implemented centralization as the Tang Dynasty. It was called Taika Reform. At this time, Silla (Korea) was very strong and was a big threat to Japan. In August 663 AD, Japan invaded Silla. At Baekgang, Tang Dynasty's navy defeated Japaese navy badly. [4]

Nara Era: From 710 to 794 AD. Power was centralized and nation was prospering. The culture exchanges between China and Japan were frequent. Japan sent many people to China. During this era, Buddhism was very popular, but the temples were corrupt, involved in politics. It also set national institute to teach Confucianism, law, Chinese, and literature, but only for nobles and officials, not for ordinary people. Government gave land to people per Bantian system [from Tang Dynasty], but peasant's life was poor. Many people ran away. Government started to let people own land. It started the manor system. Many peasants went to work for the landlord of manor. Japanese law system divided people to different status – good or cheap. [3]

Heian Era: From 794 to 1185 AD. Emperor moved the capital to Heian-kyo (now Kyoto). Japanese law system was broken, and manor system was prevailed. There were problems of local law and order. Manor owner started to set up their private army. The warrior class started to appear. The power of manor owners, warriors, and temples with monk soldiers gradually became strong. In 894 AD, stopped sending students to China. From the later part of 10th century to 11th century, nation's power fell into two high officials, Sessho and Kampaku. Later, the Pure Land Buddhism became popular in Japan. It combined with the Japan's traditional Shinto. In politics, Warrior Ping and Yuan Lai was in power one after the other. Warrior Ping rule the nation based on manors, caused resentment of other warriors and unrest in the nation.

II.1.2 Middle stage (12th – 16th century)

Kamakura Shogunate: 1185-1333. Yuan Lai was in power and set up the 1st Shogunate regime (Kamakur Shogunate). The special feature of Shogunate regime was the nation's power was in the hand of the leader of warriors. He dispatched officials (royal family [warrior]; guardian or the land master [also warrior]) to every place to manage local affairs. Emperor was a ruler by name, no power. At the beginning, manors and nobles were still very powerful. After Yuan Lai died, Hojo was in power. Mongolia attacked Japan twice, but failed. At the meantime, local officials started dislike the ruling of Shogunate. Peasants' power greatly increased. They started to fight against the exploitation of manors. Buddhism was simplified and accepted by warriors and the multitudes. Later, royal family and warriors united together and overthrew Hojo.

Muromachi Shogunate: 1333-1477. After Kamakur Shogunate, emperor ruled Japan for several years. He protected manor owners, but he was quickly stopped by warriors. Emperor fled to the south. Ashikaga established Muromachi Shogunate at the north, started the 60 year of South-North Dynasty. At this time, many local leaders (Daming) became stronger than the manors. They helped Muromachi Shogunate defeated the South Dynasty united Japan. Muromachi Shogunate planned to reduce local leaders's power but failed. At this time, everywhere people were against the government, but the Shogunate was not able to stop them and local leaders' power became stronger.

The Warring States Era: 1477-1547. After Yingren Chaos (1467-1477), Muromachi Shogunate lost its power. Japan entered the unrest Warring States Era. The nation was ruled by many local leaders.

II.1.3 Late stage (16th to mid-19th century)

Antu Taoshan Era (also named Anzuchi Momoyama Era): 1547-1603. Later, Oda Nobunaga, a local leader, consolidated the chaos of the Warring States, perished Muromachi Shogunate, dissolved the army of temples, and almost united Japan, but he committed suicide during a rebellion. Toyotomi Hideyoshi took over and united Japan. He issued an order of knife control and an order of land survey, which had big effect later, but he didn't establish a good pollical system. Therefore, after he died, the government went downhill. Toyotomi Hideyoshi invaded Korea (1592-1598) but was defeated by Ming Dynasty. [4]

Tokugawa Shogunate: 1603-1876. Tokugawa Ieyasu was in power, established Tokugawa Shogunate. It was also called Edo Era. It was a feudal government. The central government was ruled by Shogunate, and the local government was ruled by a local leader. For the convenient of ruling, people were divided into 5 groups. It took a policy not to contact with other nations. During this period, economic was quickly developed, but warriors and peasants were even poorer. Later, it faced the problems of financial difficulties, peasants' riots, and movement to respect emperor and anti-foreigner. Besides these problems, foreign nations demanded to open trade with Japan. It was forced to sign unequal treaties (such as the most favorable nation treatment, foreigner's jurisdiction right). Due to popularization of education and business development, ordinary people and businessman started to enter the stage of the history. At last, the 15th generation of General returned the power to the Emperor. During Edo Era, Rangaku was developed through Dutch. It was basically knowledge of western science. It helped later in Japan's modernization.

II.2 Japan Empire (mid-19th to mid-20th century)

Meiji Reform: 1868-1912. When Emperor Meiji was in power, he implemented westernization policy, which greater increased Japan's power. He established a constitutional monarchy. In 1889, Japan published the 1st Asian constitution, the Great Japanese Empire Constitution. He abolished unequal treaties and let Japan be the only nation in Asia able to keep independent in the 19th century. Japan became a capitalism nation. When it became stronger, it adopted imperialism. In 1879, it annexed Ryukyu Kingdom by force. In 1895, Japan defeated China in the Sino-Japan War. It gained Taiwan and Penghu Islands, became the 1st strong nation in Asia. In 1905, Japan defeated Russa, gained lease right at Guangdong area, gained south of Sakhalin, and became protectorate of Korea. In 1910, Japan annexed Korea by force.

Invaded China and Asia: On September 18, 1931, Japan launched 918 Incident, took Manchuria; on July 7, 1937, launched Lugouqiao Incident, started the Sino-Japan War; in September 1940, attacked Indochina. In December 1941, Japan launched Peral Harbor Attack and USA declared war against Japan. In June 1942, Japan failed in attacking Midway Island and started its way to be defeated. In June 1944, American navy and Japanese navy fought a large scale war at the Philipines Sea. Japan was defeated. In August 1945, USA dropped two atomic bombs at Japan. Japan surrendered.

II.3 Japan after WWII (mid-20th century to now (August 2019))

After WWII, Japan was occupied by USA. American policy was to transform Japan with non-militaryism and democracy. Actual practices were: abolished Emperor's political power, dissolved troop, arrested war criminals, deprived Militaryism leader and officers position; dissolved financial magnates; implemented land reform; labor reform; formulating new constitution; promoting democracy, etc.; reformed Japan's politics, economic, society, and culture. It paved the foundation for Japan's politics and economy after the war.

After WWII, the relation between USA and Soviet Union worsened. It started the cold war. USA's policy also revised to actively help Japan recover and rearm Japan to let Japan be an ally. In 1952, USA returned the ruling power back to Japan.

Japan developed its economic. Now, it is a big economic nation in the world. Japan also develop its military forces, hope to become a big military nation. Japan plans to revise its constitution, so that it will be allowed to further develop its military strength.

III. Some thought

From Japanese history, we see the sinful nature of human. After Japan became strong, it didn't try to help its neighbor, but tried invasion to gain more wealth. Besides this, Japan also killed neighboring nation's people, raped their women. Japan had no justice and moral. After WWII, Japan was very lucky, didn't pay compensation to invaded nations, and continued occupied Okinawa. Besides these, Japan hoped to gain more land. Japan does not repent about its mistakes and still hope to be a big military power.

Japanese are obedient to authority. Japan's royal family can last 1600 years. It is a rare event in the world. Obedience to authority has good and bad points. The good one is easy for the government to manage its people. The bad one is if the government was bad, people are help it to do bad thing, without justice.

In fact, Japan's future is not to be a big economic or military power. Japan's future is at peace with its neighbor, because Japan has limited population and resources. Japan doesn't have the assets to be a big power. In fact, the goal of any nation should be to keep its people to live happily, peaceful with other nations, and be justice.

IV. God's word [Bible verses from New Testament (Standard version)]

Romans 6:23 For the wages of sin is death, but the free gift of God is eternal life in Christ Jesus our Lord.
Romans 10:10-11 For with the heart one believes and is justified, and with the mouth one confesses and is saved. For the Scripture says, "Everyone who believes in him will not be put to shame."

Notes:
1. The origin of Japanese; see website:
https://wenku.baidu.com/view/f2fa18e3b8f67c1cfad6b819.html?rec_flag=default&sxts=1563889622255
https://wenku.baidu.com/view/920735740a4e767f5acfa1c7aa00b52acfc79cfd.html?from=search
2. Japaese history; see website:
https://wenku.baidu.com/view/20cce5180975f46526d3e14b.html?from=search;
https://en.wikipedia.org/wiki/History_of_Japan
3. Japan's ancient law system; see website:
https://wenku.baidu.com/view/d0981afb941ea76e58fa0461.html?from=search
4. Five Sino-Japan War; see website:
https://wenku.baidu.com/view/7e332ff7f424ccbff121dd36a32d7375a417c62d.html?from=search

Chapter 6 God's Kingdom

After we see the history of China, USA, and Japan, we see there is no justice in this world, but force. A weak country has no say in its foreign diplomacy. This is due to the sinful human nature. But when God made human, He gives us conscience. Therefore, we still see the struggle of justice in our history. For the people who know God, it is clear that the fate of the world and human is not in our hand, but God, because He is more powerful than us. No matter you know God or not, we are under His authority.

In Chapter 2, we already did analysis, as long as sinful nature of human exists, the criteria to judge a nation should not based on the system of its government, capitalism or socialism, democracy or autocracy, but on whether it is really serving its people and seek peace for the world. In this chapter, we will see the God's plan for human, God's kingdom.

I. Who is God

God is a spirit. He is the creator and the ruler of the universe. Among all the gods in this world, only this God told us He created the universe. From Bible, we learn there is only one God. God exists in three persons, God the Father, God the Son, and God the Holy Spirit. God the Son is Jesus. God the Holy Spirit will help us understand, remember God's teaching, and direct our behaviour. God is holy, love, justice, faithful, and merciful. God exists everywhere, knows everything, and is capable to do anything. We should (have to) know God, because 1) He is the real God, 2) He is our origin (creator), 3) He can help us to live a meaningful life, 4) only through God(Jesus), we can have eternal life (return to God).

Bible is God's word for human. Reading Bible will help us understand God, ourselves, how to life, and the future of this world. Basically, Bible teaches us two things: how to worship God and how to behave (love, forgive, and justice).

From Bible, we see God will reward the good and punish the evil. God is not a "yes" man. God doesn't like evil and false god. Through 6-7 hundred years, God tolerated the evil deeds and the false gods of Canaanites. Later, God raised Israelites to conquer Canaan, slaughtered Canaanites. Israelites didn't worship God by heart. God let them lose their country. He raised Babylon to rule over Israelites. Babylonian treated Israelites cruelly. God let them perish. God is in control of our history, human, and the universe. When will people recognize this fact? God raised a person or a nation to work for Him, not to do evil. If we do evil, God will punish us.

In Old Testament of Bible, the Book of 1 Samuel, verse 16:7 has following description. When Samuel went to the house of Jessie to select the king of

Israel to replace Saul per God's command, God told Samuel: "…For the Lord sees not as man sees; man looks on the outward appearance, but the Lord looks on the heart." God is concerned more about what we think than our appearance.

In Old Testament of Bible, the Book of Numbers, Chapter 13, it has following description. Israelites sent 12 spies to investigate the conditions of Canaan. The result: All 12 spies agreed Canaan was a nice place to live. But 10 of them were against to take the land, because they saw the local people were tall and strong and their city had strong walls. Only 2 of them wanted to take the land, because they believed God would help them. In Chapter 14, multitudes of Israel complained to Moses. In verses 14:11-12, God told Moses, "How long will this people despise me? And how long will they not believe in me, in spite of all the signs that I have done among them? I will strike them with the pestilence and disinherit them, and I will make of you a nation greater and mightier than they." Moses begged the favor for Israelites. Then, God changed His mind, not to perish Israelites. This event let us see God listens to our prayer and will accept our reasonable request.

Many people still do not know God. Even those who claim they know God do not fully know God. Most people do not respect God enough, because of the sinful human nature, selfish, and caring too much for ourselves. We should learn how to worship and serve God, not ourselves.

II. God's Salvation

Two thousand years ago, Jesus came to our world. He died on the cross for our sin. Three days later, he resurrected, defeated the death and Satan's power. Jesus prepared the salvation for human to be good with God again, a very simple method. If we accept Jesus and His Salvation, we will be God's children and able to return to God's kingdom.

III. God's prophecy

Bible told us one day Jesus will come to our world again. Bible told us about what will happen in the future as follows: Christians will be bought to heaven (Rupture). On earth, there will be seven years calamity (Tribulation). Jesus will come again. He will rule the world for one thousand years. Then, Satan will be thrown into the lake of fire disappeared forever. Then, all the unbelievers will be judged by Jesus (a white throne judgment). Finally, a new world without sin will be formed. God will give everyone a new heart. Everyone will know God. Human will live happily with God again. This is God's prophecy: tell us the future and His kingdom – from the end of the world to His new world. [1]

In Bible, there are warnings about the end of the world. In New Testament,

Gospel of Matthew, Chapter 24 has following verses: [pay attention to the underlined]

¹ Jesus left the Temple area and was walking away. But his followers came to him to show him the Temple's buildings.

² He asked them, "Are you looking at these buildings? The fact is, they will be destroyed. Every stone will be thrown down to the ground. Not one stone will be left on another."

³ Later, Jesus was sitting at a place on the Mount of Olives. The followers came to be alone with him. They said, "Tell us when these things will happen. And what will happen to prepare us for your coming and the end of time?"

⁴ Jesus answered, "Be careful! Don't let anyone fool you.

⁵ Many people will come and use my name. They will say, 'I am the Christ.' And they will fool many people.

⁶ You will hear about wars that are being fought. And you will hear stories about other wars beginning. But don't be afraid. These things must happen before the end comes.

⁷ Nations will fight against other nations. Kingdoms will fight against other kingdoms. There will be times when there is no food for people to eat. And there will be earthquakes in different places.

⁸ These things are only the beginning of troubles, like the first pains of a woman giving birth.

⁹ "Then you will be arrested and handed over to be punished and killed. People all over the world will hate you because you believe in me.

¹⁰ During that time many believers will lose their faith. They will turn against each other and hate each other.

¹¹ Many false prophets will come. They will cause many people to believe wrong things.

¹² There will be more and more evil in the world. So most believers will stop showing love.

¹³ But the one who remains faithful to the end will be saved.

¹⁴ The Good News about God's kingdom will be told in the whole world. It will be told to every nation. Then the end will come.

¹⁵ "Daniel the prophet spoke about 'the terrible thing that causes destruction.' You will see this terrible thing standing in the holy place." (You who read this should understand what it means.) …

²¹ because it will be a time of great trouble. There will be more trouble than has ever happened since the beginning of the world. And nothing as bad as that will ever happen again.

²² "But God has decided to make that terrible time short. If it were not made short, no one would continue living. But God will make that time short to help the people he has chosen.

²³ "Someone might say to you at that time, 'Look, there is the Christ!' Or someone else might say, 'There he is!' But don't believe them.

[24] False Christs and false prophets will come and do great miracles and wonders, trying to fool the people God has chosen, if that is possible.
[25] Now I have warned you about this before it happens.
[26] "Someone might tell you, 'The Christ is there in the desert!' But don't go into the desert to look for him. Someone else might say, 'There is the Christ in that room!' But don't believe it.
[27] When the Son of Man comes, everyone will see him. It will be like lightning flashing in the sky that can be seen everywhere.
[28] It's like looking for a dead body: You will find it where the vultures are gathering above.
[29] "Right after the trouble of those days, this will happen: 'The sun will become dark, and the moon will not give light. The stars will fall from the sky, and everything in the sky will be changed.'
[30] "Then there will be something in the sky that shows the Son of Man is coming. All the people of the world will cry. Everyone will see the Son of Man coming on the clouds in the sky. He will come with power and great glory.
[31] He will use a loud trumpet to send his angels all around the earth. They will gather his chosen people from every part of the earth.
[32] "The fig tree teaches us a lesson: When its branches become green and soft, and new leaves begin to grow, then you know that summer is near.
[33] In the same way, when you see all these things happening, you will know that the time is near, ready to come.
[34] I assure you that all these things will happen while some of the people of this time are still living.
[35] The whole world, earth and sky, will be destroyed, but my words will last forever.
[36] "No one knows when that day or time will be. The Son and the angels in heaven don't know when it will be. Only the Father knows.

From the Bible verses above, we see the omens for the upcoming of the end of the world: Gospel will be spread all over the world. The beginning of the end: appear of false Christ, wars, famines, plagues, and earthquakes. Tribulation happens. Appear of false Christ and prophets, their miracles, and confused people. After Tribulation, the sun will become dark, the moom wil not give light, and the stars will fall from the sky. Jesus will come again, descending from the sky. But no one will know the date, except God the Father. In the Book of Revelation, New Testament, it also mentions that during Tribulation, anti-Christ will appear. During the last 3.5 years of the Tribulation, he will suppress Christians.

IV. The Ten Commandments [2]

Three months after Moses led Israelites left Egypt, they arrived Mount Sinai. At Mount Sinai, God appeared to Israelites, gave Moses the Ten Commandments written on two stone tablets, asked Moses to teach

Israelites how to behave based on these commandments. These Ten Commandments were also given us from God. They are: 1. Besides God, there is no other god. 2. Don't worship idols. 3. Don't misuse God's name. 4. Keep the Sabbath day holly. [3] 5. Honor your parents. 6. You shall not murder. 7. You shall not commit adultery. 8. You shall not steal. 9. You shall not make false testimony. 10. You shall not covet other's properties.

V. God's word [Bible verses from New Testament (ERV)]

John 14:6 Jesus answered, "I am the way, the truth, and the life. The only way to the Father is through me.
Matthew 28:19-20 So go and make followers of all people in the world. Baptize them in the name of the Father and the Son and the Holy Spirit. Teach them to obey everything that I have told you. You can be sure that I will be with you always. I will continue with you until the end of time."
2 Peter 3:9 The Lord is not being slow in doing what he promised - the way some people understand slowness. But God is being patient with you. He doesn't want anyone to be lost. He wants everyone to change their ways and stop sinning.
Matthew 11:28 "Come to me all of you who are tired from the heavy burden you have been forced to carry. I will give you rest.

Lord's prayer [Jesus Christ teaches people how to pray.] Matthew 6:9-13 [Bible verses from New Testament (ESV)]

[9] Pray then like this: "Our Father in heaven, hallowed be your name.
[10] Your kingdom come, your will be done, on earth as it is in heaven.
[11] Give us this day our daily bread,
[12] and forgive us our debts, as we also have forgiven our debtors.
[13] And lead us not into temptation but deliver us from evil."

Notes:
1. See New Testament, the Book of Revelation. Christians will be taken to heaven [Rupture]. There are three explanation about its timing: before, in the middle of, and after Tribulation.
2. See Old Testament, Exodus 20:16-21. Besides Ten Commandments, God also gives us other rules about how to worship Him and how to behave in the Book of Leviticus, the Book of Numbers, and the Book of Deuteronomy.
3. Sabbath Day was on Saturday. Now, Christians use Sunday as Sabbath Day and also use Sunday to worship God.

www.ingramcontent.com/pod-product-compliance
Lightning Source LLC
Chambersburg PA
CBHW051355280526
45784CB00007B/2970